ENGLISH DEPT.
ABERDEEN GRAMMAR SCHOOL

General Editor: Aidan Chambers

THE CRANE

The town council builds the tallest crane in the world and puts it in the charge of a young man with a blue feather in his cap. He climbs to the driver's cabin at the top and stays there. From his perch he watches the town change, a war come and go, a flood sweep in to cover the land. Then he is alone except for his friend, the eagle. All the time he keeps the crane in working order till the disasters are over and a new world grows up beneath him. But by then the crane driver is getting old and tired: time for him to move on.

Reiner Zimnik was born in 1930 in Poland. At the end of the Second World War, he settled in Germany in Munich, where he works as a writer and artist. He says he likes nature, a simple life and ordinary people.

M Books is a series consisting of some of the best contemporary fiction for young people. Other titles you may enjoy are

The Day of the Pigeons Roy Brown
Goodbye, Chicken Little Betsy Byars
The Cartoonist Betsy Byars
The Eighteenth Emergency Betsy Byars
The Night Swimmers Betsy Byars
The Pinballs Betsy Byars
The TV Kid Betsy Byars
Time Trap Nicholas Fisk
I Am David Anne Holm
The Jungle Book Rudyard Kipling
The Great Gilly Hopkins Katherine Paterson
The Shadow Cage Philippa Pearce
The Cats Joan Phipson
Midnite Randolph Stow
Charlotte's Web E B White
The Crane Reiner Zimnik

The Crane

Reiner Zimnik

Translated from the German by Marion Koenig

Macmillan Education

© Atrium Verlag 1956
Translation © Brockhampton Press Ltd 1969

All rights reserved. No reproduction, copy or transmission
of this publication may be made without written permission.

No paragraph of this publication may be reproduced, copied
or transmitted save with written permission or in accordance
with the provisions of the Copyright Act 1956 (as amended),
or under the terms of any licence permitting limited copying
issued by the Copyright Licensing Agency, 33—4 Alfred Place,
London WC1E 7DP.

Any person who does any unauthorised act in relation to
this publication may be liable to criminal prosecution and
civil claims for damages.

First published in Switzerland as *Der Kran* 1956
First published in Great Britain by Brockhampton Press Ltd 1969

Published in *M Books* in 1978
Reprinted 1979, 1988

Published by
MACMILLAN EDUCATION LTD
Houndmills, Basingstoke, Hampshire RG21 2XS
and London
Associated companies in Delhi Dublin
Hong Kong Johannesburg Lagos Melbourne
New York Singapore and Tokyo

Printed in Hong Kong

British Library Cataloguing in Publication Data
Zimnik, Reiner
The crane. — (M books).
I. Title II. Series III. Koenig, Marion
833'.9'IF   PZ7.Z64
ISBN 0—333—24486—9

This book is dedicated to
Professor Oberberger and Hanna Axmann

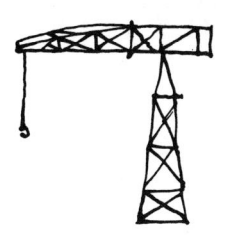

THE CRANE

The man at the end of the top row, on the right, is just the caretaker.

THE CRANE

The town got bigger and bigger, and there was no more room at the goods yard for the crates and the coal, the cows and the pigs. That is why the mayor, the town clerk and the twelve town councillors decided to build a crane outside the town to load the goods.

First of all, however, they sent off a man on a motor-bike with a folding rule. He had to visit all the big towns in the country and measure the height of the tallest cranes in the ports and the goods yards.

When he got back, he said:

'One hundred and sixty feet.'

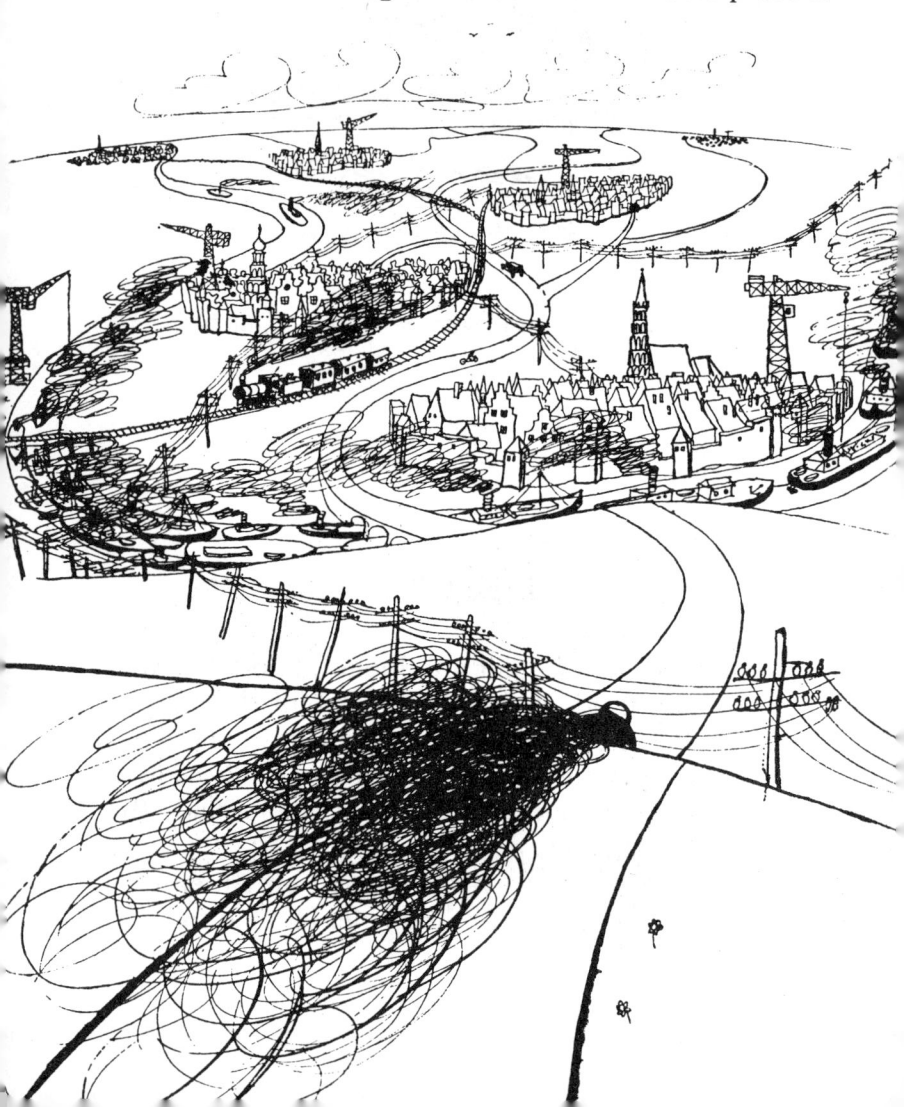

In the afternoon, the mayor, the town clerk and the twelve town councillors gathered outside the town and began to look for a suitable place to build the crane. At a place where the river, the road and the railway lines all met, they stopped. The town clerk scratched a cross in the sand with his walking-stick and said:

'It will stand here and it will be a hundred and sixty-one feet high.'

So the mayor and the town councillors looked up into the air, roughly a hundred and sixty-one feet up, and one of them said:

'Magnificent!'

Then they all returned to the town and drank whisky and beer and enjoyed themselves.

The next morning workmen arrived with hammers, rivets and screws, and lorries laden with iron girders, and they began to build the crane exactly on top of the cross which the town clerk had scratched in the sand.

They were paid two and sixpence an hour and they hammered and rivetted from morning to night. When the sun had gone down the lorry drivers switched on their headlamps and more men arrived and carried on the hammering and rivetting until the next morning.

I have drawn the town councillors flat on purpose.

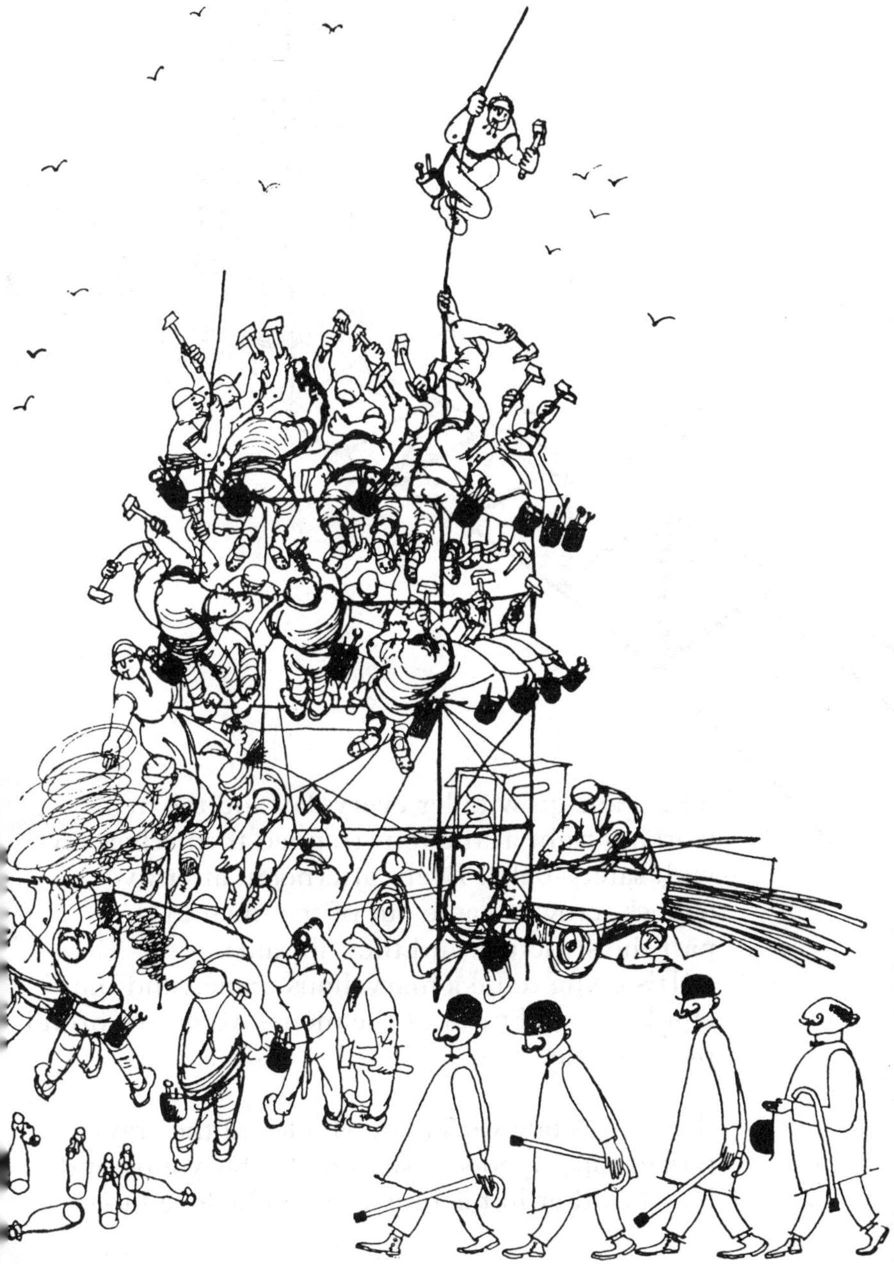

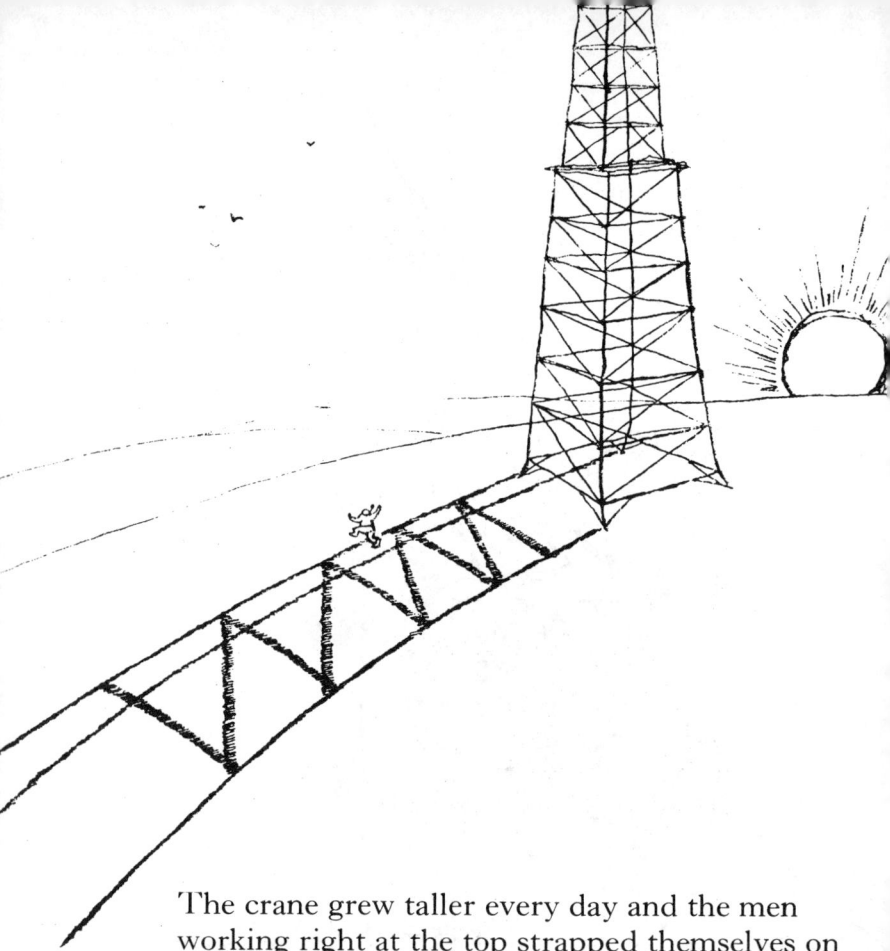

The crane grew taller every day and the men working right at the top strapped themselves on with safety-belts. Every afternoon, after five o'clock, crowds came out of the town to stroll past the structure and they all said:

'It's going to be a marvellous crane,' and the children—and most of the men—were very proud of the crane.

There was one workman who loved the crane more than anybody else did. He was young and had a feather in his blue cap and he loved the crane so much that they all said: 'He's out of his mind.' He hammered and rivetted three times faster than the other men, and when they went home at the end of the day, he climbed around at the top of the crane polishing all the screws with his handkerchief until they shone. Every night he slept under the crane. And every morning he jumped in and out of its shadow while all the others said: 'That man with the feather in his blue cap is out of his mind.'

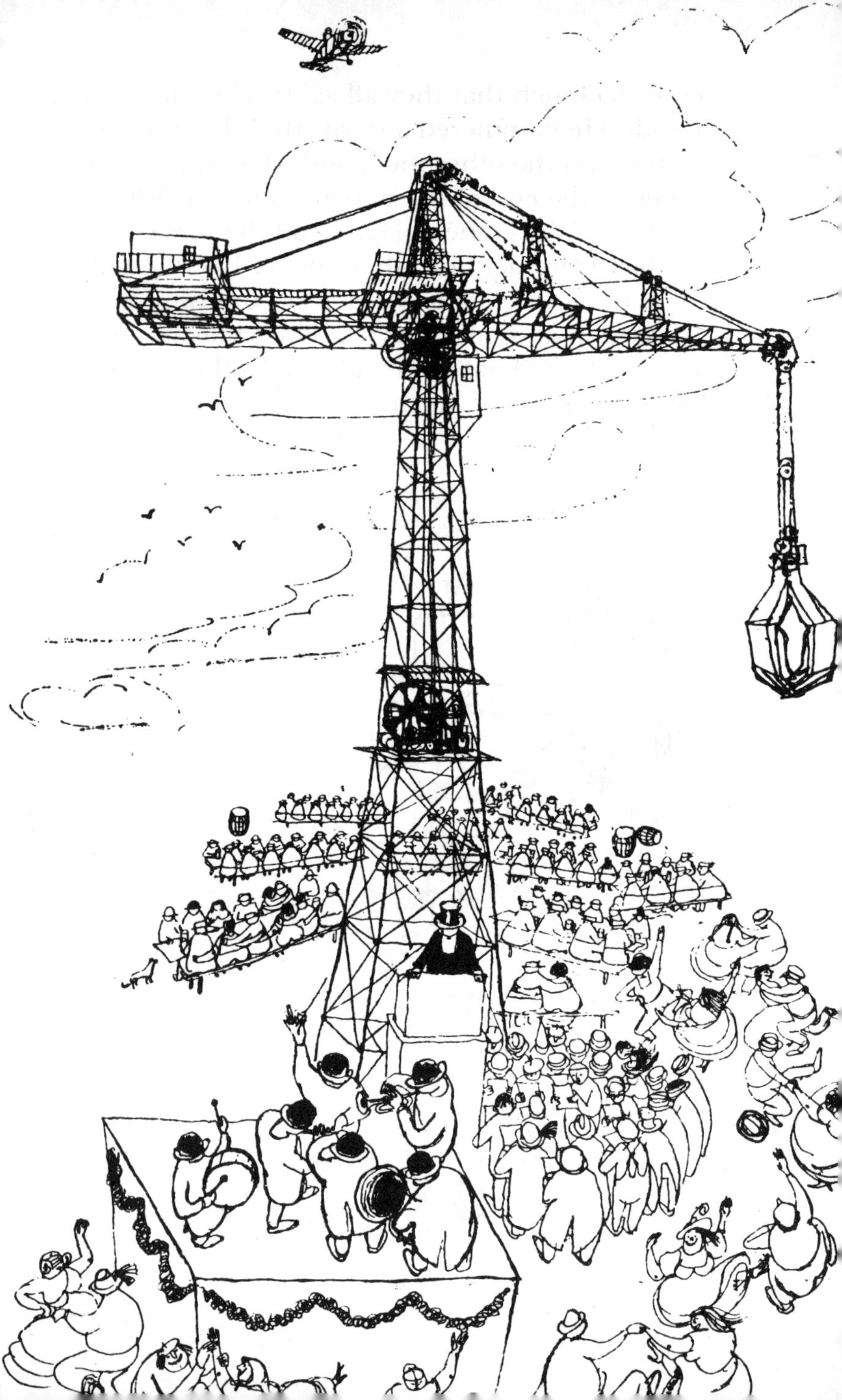

When the crane was finished, all the townsfolk gathered round it. The town clerk made a speech, the brass band played, the people drank beer and danced and milled around, joking and pelting each other with flowers. It was a great occasion and they all enjoyed themselves.

On the Monday, lorries brought crates and coal, the goods-trains and ships arrived too, all ready for loading. But the crane was useless because there was no crane driver.

The town clerk's brother-in-law wanted the job and so did a friend of the mayor, and as neither of them would give way, there was nobody to man the crane. The seamen, the guards on the goods trains and the lorry drivers were furious and shouted: 'Hey there! What about our goods?' But the crane did not move.

Suddenly the man in the blue cap climbed up the crane as nimbly as a squirrel and sat down at the controls in the cabin. While the mayor's friend and the town clerk's brother-in-law argued and called each other names down below, he swung the jib round to the right and to the left. He let the grab zoom up and down and lifted coal from the ships and loaded it into the railway trucks; he lifted the crates and cows and pigs from the railway trucks and lowered them into the lorries. He did all this as if he had done nothing else all his life.

It was marvellous to see that crane being worked: to hear the engine hum, the cog-wheels screech, the pulley clatter, the grab clank—and to see the trucks being loaded one after another. The lorry drivers, the guards and the seamen shouted:

'That man in the blue cap is a good crane driver. He's worth keeping!'

At the end of the day they all went up to the town councillors and said: 'We want that man in the blue cap as crane driver and no one else.'

The town clerk and the mayor said: 'No!' But the twelve town councillors said: 'Yes!'

They sent off a telegram which looked like this:

POST OFFICE TELEGRAM

Prefix.　Time handed in.　Office of Origin and Service Instructions.　Words.

MAN IN BLUE CAP HEREBY APPOINTED CRANE DRIVER.
PAY TWO SHILLINGS AND SIXPENCE PER HOUR.
CONDITIONS: WORKING HOURS FROM 7 A.M. TO 5
P.M. LUNCH BREAK 12 NOON TO 1 P.M. SATURDAY
AFTERNOONS OFF. SIREN TO BE SOUNDED DAILY AT
7 A.M. 12 NOON 1 P.M. AND 5 P.M. EXCEPT
SUNDAYS. ONCE A MONTH CRANE TO BE CLEANED
FILLED UP WITH PETROL AND ENGINE OILED.
TOWN COUNCILLORS TO BE LIFTED ACROSS RIVER
EVERY SUNDAY AT 10 A.M. AND 11 A.M. WORK
HARD.

　　TWELVE TOWN COUNCILLORS

The telegraph boy shouted: 'Hey! Crane driver! Come on down! Telegram from the Council!' But the man in the blue cap called back: 'I'm staying up here. Just leave it on the ground, would you?'

So the telegraph boy placed the telegram on the ground and the crane driver picked it up with the grab. He even threw down a tip for the telegraph boy. Threepence.

When the crane driver had read the telegram, he quivered with pleasure and swung up and down on the iron girders like a monkey. He then felt quite hot and said to himself: 'It's nothing to get steamed up about.'

But later on, when the moon stood high over the fields, he remembered the town clerk's brother-in-law and the mayor's friend and that they might come to get him down off the crane. So he dismantled the ladder and watched out for them.

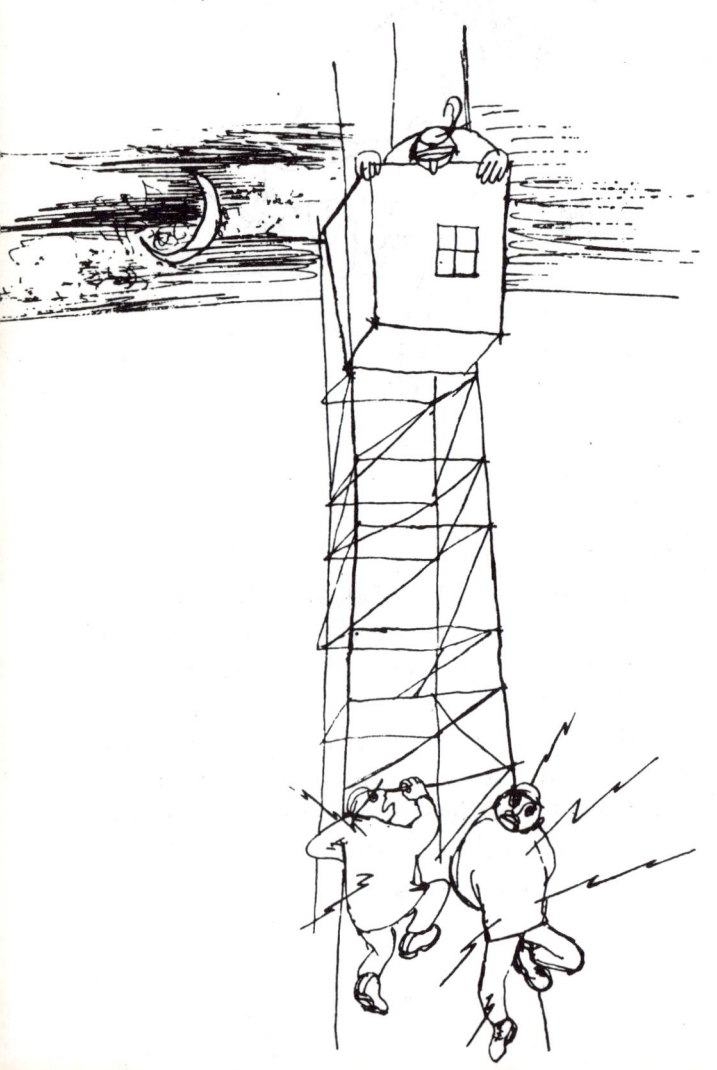

And after it had struck twelve o'clock, he saw two shadowy forms creeping towards the crane. He leaped quickly on to the roof of the cabin (made of insulated tar-board) and directed a strong electric current from the machine through the metal framework of the crane. The town clerk's brother-in-law and the mayor's friend had already climbed ten feet when the current gave them such a shock that it almost killed them. They crossed themselves and swore they would never again attempt to climb up a crane.

After that the crane driver lay down, high up on the crane, and felt happy. He saw the stars far above him in the sky and the mountain in the distance and he felt so happy that he could not sleep.

He whistled 'Loch Lomond' all night long, drumming his heels on the iron girders, and looked forward to the next day.

The night-watchman could not stand the whistling for he was musical. He shouted up to the crane driver:

'Oy! Why don't you shut up and go to sleep like a respectable Christian?'

But the crane driver shouted down: 'Don't mind me! I'm happy!' So the night-watchman shouted up again: 'Well, save it for tomorrow then!' And thought: 'Fool!'

At dawn, the crane driver rolled up his sleeves and shouted down: 'Hi! Is it nearly seven yet?' But it was only half-past four. The crane driver paced up and down on the crane impatiently and the night-watchman was very annoyed because every five minutes the crane driver kept shouting down: 'Hi! Is it nearly seven yet?'

Burglars are not usually out and about in daylight, which is why night-watchmen generally drop off to sleep at dawn. But if someone keeps shouting: 'Hi! Is it nearly seven yet?' every five minutes, no night-watchmen can get any rest.

As it got lighter and lighter, the crane driver spat into his hands. At half-past five a dog ran by below. At six o'clock the bell of a tram in the town could be heard; at half-past six the farmers drove loads of manure out into the fields—but it was not seven till seven.

The crane driver yelled: 'Here we go!' and sounded the siren. The engine hummed, the lorries rumbled, the pulley clattered, the loads swayed through the air, the sun shone and everyone was happy.

At half-past ten an electric truck arrived with twelve trailers full of parcels. It was driven by the crane driver's friend. His nickname was Lektro. He was the best electric truck driver for miles around. No one could manoeuvre a truck

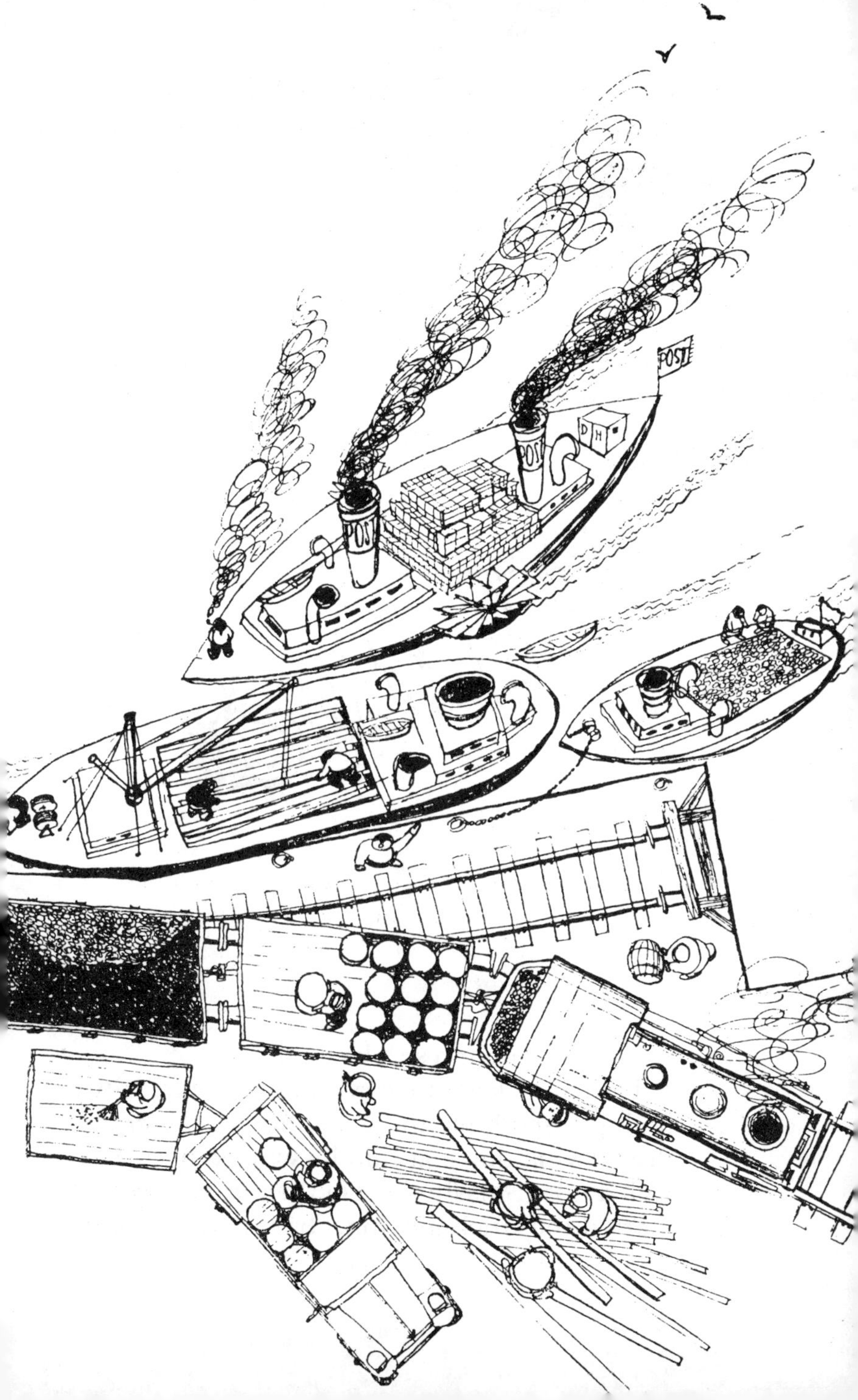
POST
POST
POST
DH

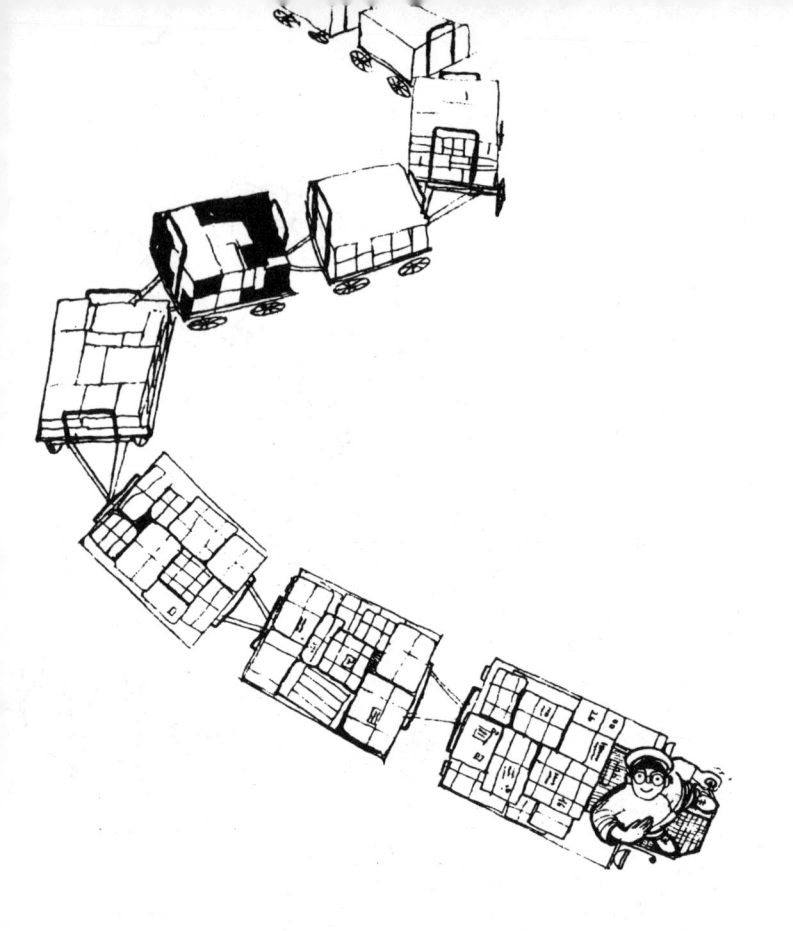

in such tight curves as he could.

Lektro looked at everything very carefully and it all pleased him, and when he saw the crane driver wink down at him he winked back and called up: 'Smashing!' He then waved and started the truck moving. Rrrr whee! it went. It always went Rrrr whee! when he switched on the current. And Lektro whistled 'Loch Lomond'.

The man with the ox team was Lektro's brother. He was very calm and never in a hurry. Originally he had been apprenticed to a hairdresser. And every month he would cut Lektro's hair and that of the crane driver free of charge.

At midday the crane driver sounded the siren again and threw down a scrap of paper on which he had listed the things he wanted the lorry drivers to buy for him: bread, beer, shaving soap and peppermints. Peppermints were his favourite sweets. He also threw down some money wrapped up in paper.

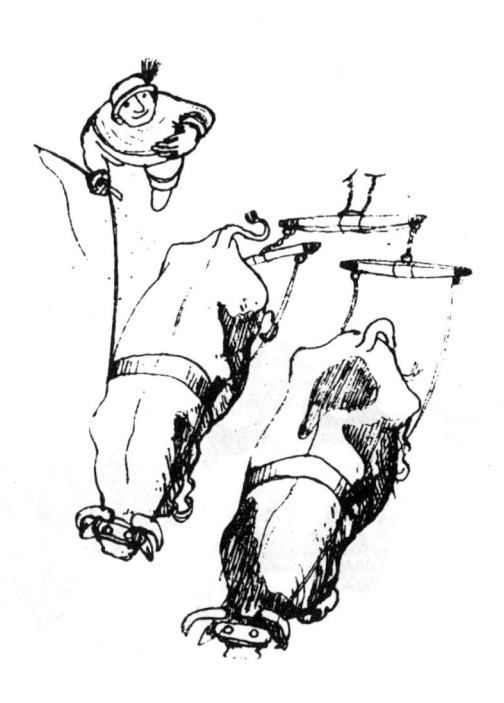

When he needed water, he scooped it out of the river with the grab—and as he only washed once a day, he did not need very much.

The crane, the river down below, the ships, and the way the iron girders hummed when a light breeze blew from the town, the stars at night, the fact that he could see everything from up there—it was like a wonderful dream, but he knew it was even better because it was real.

On Sunday mornings he unscrewed the machinery and cleaned the fly-wheels with petrol. When he had finished, he very carefully oiled all the parts.

And on Sunday mornings the twelve town councillors would appear. Every Sunday morn-

After you, Sir, after you.

ing they went for a walk together because the town hall was closed on that day. One of them collected butterflies. The town councillors would climb into a large box with flowers and birds painted on it. They did not have to stand because there were seats in the box, which had been upholstered with red velvet. The crane driver's job was to lift the box containing the twelve town councillors across the river. They would have preferred to build a bridge, but the opposite bank belonged to strangers who did not want one.

On Sunday afternoons the crane driver would put on his swimming trunks and sunbathe.

The girls from the bakery would put on powder and lipstick and go for a stroll. On passing the crane they would smile and wave for they liked the crane driver and they would have liked to marry him. They would call up:

'Come on down and dance with us.'

But the crane driver called back: 'They're all jealous of me. They all want to be crane drivers. Maybe one of them's digging a ditch and camouflaging it with twigs and moss. If I came down and fell into it someone else would become crane driver. Thanks all the same, but I'd rather stay up here.'

He sucked one of his peppermints and went on lying in the sun.

Lektro was a slow thinker, but he was thorough. Whenever he wanted to work out something he had to sit down and drink stout.

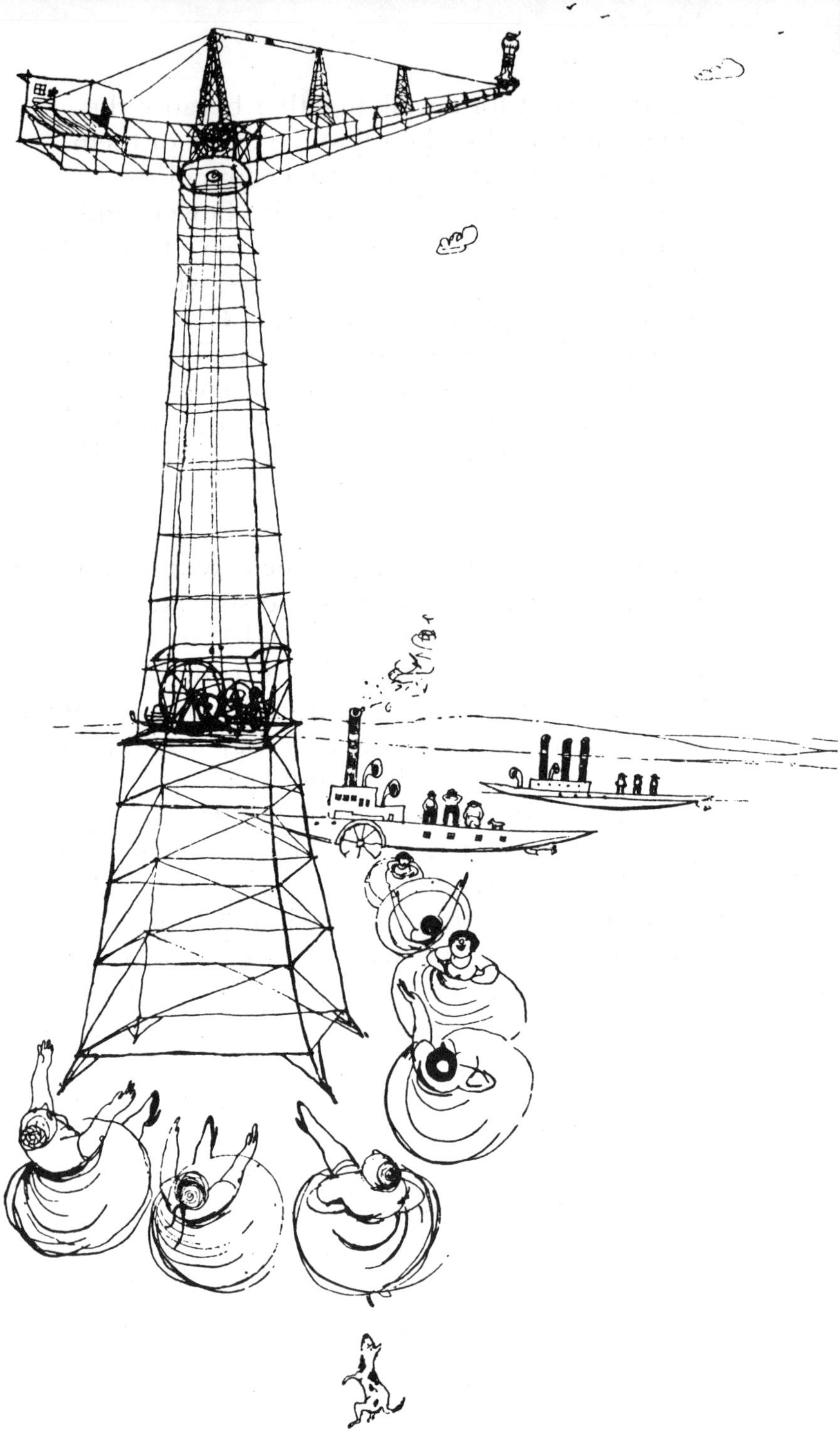

Lektro in the country (daydreaming)

In summertime, when the warm air shimmered as the grasshoppers jumped from flower to flower, his head would be full of daydreams. On such days Lektro would leave his truck at the side of the road and wander off to sit among the flowers, watching the clouds float past and enjoying his daydreams. Passing lorry drivers would shout: 'Oy, Lektro! Anything wrong?' And Lektro would reply: 'Nothing much. Just a puncture.'

Lektro visited his friend every day. He would call up: 'Chuck us one!' And they would each suck a peppermint and enjoy each other's company. Sometimes he would bring a flower with him, and whenever the truck ran out of juice he would say to the crane driver: 'Lend us a couple of kilowatts!' Then the crane driver would throw down a cable and recharge Lektro's batteries for him. As he drove away again Lektro would call out: 'So long, old pal.' Rrrr whee!

One day the crane driver had to unload a circus train. It was a very hot day. At lunch-time the iron girders were hot enough to burn one's fingers. By three o'clock on that afternoon it was as hot as Africa. The lions and tigers and all the other animals thought of jungle and desert and became quite unmanageable. They raged and roared and hurled themselves with all their might against the doors of the cages and the locks loosened. Their howling and roaring sounded like hell on earth, and the keepers trembled and hid in empty tar barrels. Finally a trumpeting, snorting and thundering was heard which sounded as if the devil himself had broken loose, and the keepers cried out in desperation: 'Holy St Castulus, save us!' They crouched even lower in their barrels and thought their last hour had come. And then, charging across the loading site came, not the devil himself, but the elephant. That was just as bad,

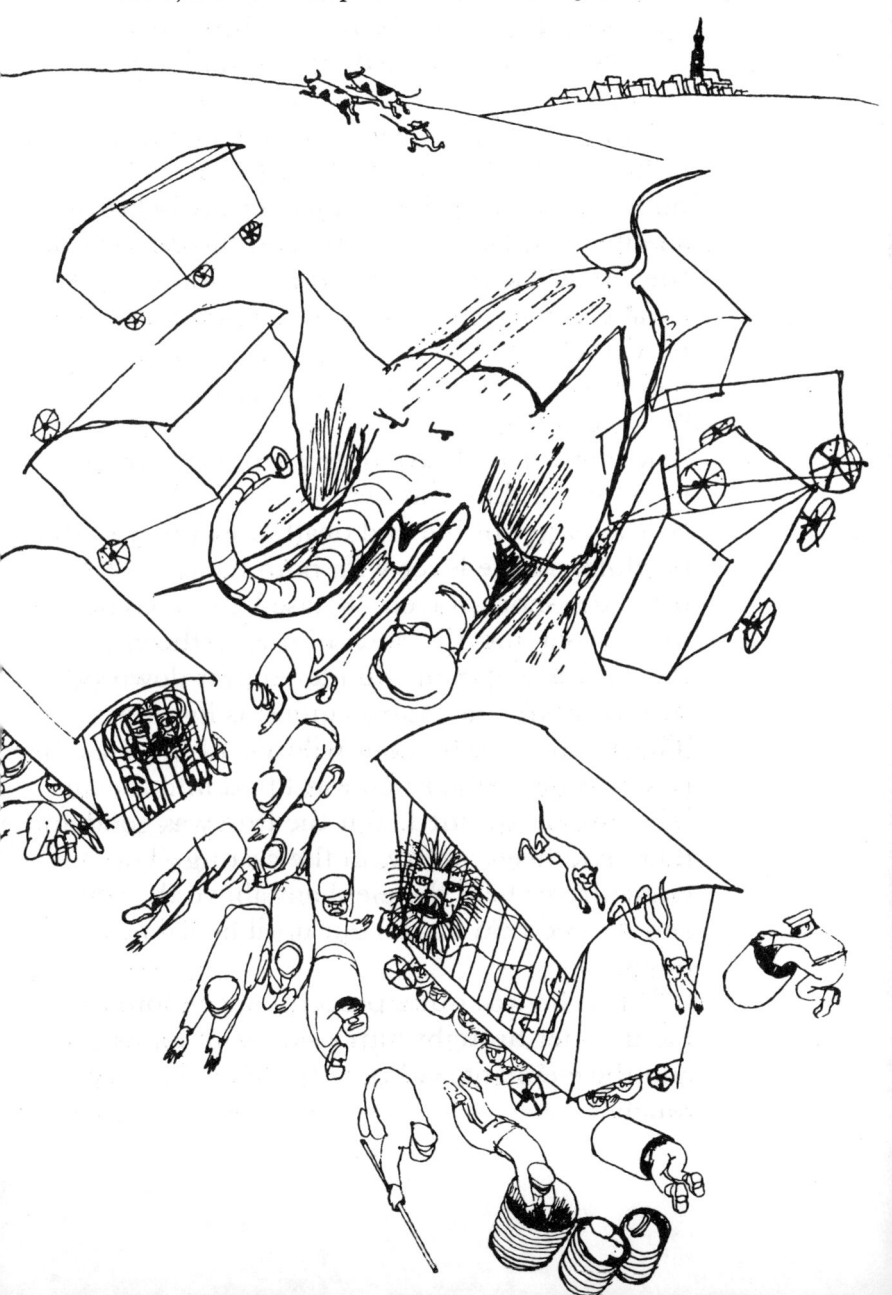

however, because he had sunstroke. He knocked over the trucks, trampled the engines, and hurled crates, cows and pigs into the air as if they were toys. The man with the ox team drove away his oxen as quickly as he could, for they belonged to him. A circus rider called: 'Come on, Jumbo, calm down, and we'll give you a bunch of bananas.' But the elephant took no notice. He got wilder and wilder till Lektro shouted: 'Better get a gun,' and the director of the circus shouted even louder: 'Don't shoot! That elephant cost five thousand pounds.' By now, the hinges on the doors of the lion's cages had worked very loose indeed.

The crane driver saw all this from the top of the crane and he was very worried. He thought: 'It's a matter of life and death down there.' So he clutched the lever with both hands and uttered a short prayer: 'Please let him come a little closer and I'll catch him with the grab.' And as the elephant thundered past down below he sent down the grab as quick as lightning. The elephant lashed out wildly with his legs, his ears and his trunk as he was lifted into the air. The girders strained. But the iron was good and there had been no flaw in the casting. The crane driver held the elephant above the water and dipped him in and out until he calmed down.

When he was quite peaceful once more the circus rider brought him a bunch of bananas and the elephant said quietly: 'Thanks very much.'

He then walked along the cages slowly and said to the animals: 'Calm down. We're not in Africa now. It's just very hot today.' And when some of them still would not believe him, he blew sawdust in their faces—particularly the lions.

By the time the town fire-engine raced up, and the policemen with guns appeared, all the animals were fast asleep in their cages. The crane driver was busily loading goods and sucking a peppermint while the circus director wiped the sweat off his forehead with a green handkerchief and said: 'Everything under control. It was only the heat.'

Only Lektro was still upset. He had to have five imaginary punctures that day. He also drove all over the town shouting: 'I saw it all. I saw the whole thing.' And when twenty people had collected round him, all asking: 'What's the matter? What did you see?' he would tell them about it. 'An elephant, as big as a house, weighing at least ten tons—the crane driver picked him up with the grab, like this, like a sack of flour.' He would show how the crane driver had picked up the elephant in the grab. 'And the girders strained under the weight. It was terrific. He's saved all our lives. The animals all had sunstroke. They would have escaped and overrun the town. The elephant would have battered down the doors—imagine coming home tired from the office and finding a hungry African lion lurking on the first-floor landing, like this.' Lektro would crouch down and gnash his teeth like a lion. The crowd got such a vivid impression of what it might have been like that they shook with fright and held on to each other's hands.

From then on everybody would always look carefully to make sure that no lion lurked on the landing whenever they got home late.

That same evening the townsfolk gathered round the crane to thank the crane driver. The girls from the bakery wanted to give him a bunch of flowers, but they couldn't throw it high enough, so the crane driver sent down the grab and the crowd packed it full of yellow flowers.

The crane driver was very happy. He whistled

'Loch Lomond' and threw down three apples and the rest of his peppermints to the people below. And at the end of it all the crowd gave him three cheers.

When Lektro came home late the following evening, he saw a silver lion on the landing and he told people what he had seen.

Two postmen, however, went to the town councillors and said: 'Lektro says he has five punctures a day, although his truck has solid tyres. He spends his time daydreaming among the flowers and just pretends he's had a puncture.'

So the town councillors sent for Lektro and one of them said:

'We understand that whenever you want to go daydreaming among the flowers you pretend to have a puncture. What is more, we are told that this happens five times a day. Is this true?'

Lektro said: 'No.'

The town councillors said: 'You're lying.'

Then Lektro said: 'Not five times a day. Twice at the most. And never in winter.'

'And you've been telling people that you saw a silver lion on the landing. Is that true?'

'Yes,' said Lektro. 'But it didn't do anything. It didn't dare. It ran away.'

'You're lying,' the town councillors said again. 'There's no such thing as a lion that doesn't dare.'

Whereupon they told Lektro they did not require his services any more, starting from the following Saturday.

Lektro drove slowly to the crane and called: 'I've been sacked. I'm to stop work on Saturday.' Rrrr whee! He was very unhappy.

The crane driver waited until the following Sunday. When he was lifting the town councillors over the river, he waited until the box was right over the water and then pulled the lever over so that the crane stopped moving. After that he moved the lever in a different way

The sacking of Lektro

so that the crane swung backwards and forwards just a little. And the box began to rock to the right and left—quite slowly at first, but getting faster. The town councillors got very uneasy and they called out: 'What's happening?'

The crane driver crept along the arm of the crane until he got as far as the grab and shouted: 'There's a connection loose in the electrical system.'

The river was a long way down. The box rocked to and fro wildly and the town councillors had all had eggs and bacon for breakfast.

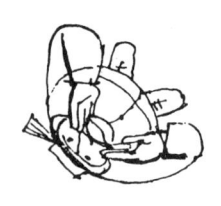

The town councillors shouted: 'Get it mended immediately!'

The crane driver said: 'Those aren't swing ropes. They'll soon give.' And the man with the ox team stood on the shore. He made a trumpet of his hands and shouted: 'They'll go any moment.'

One of the councillors shouted: 'I can swim, I can swim.' But the others could not swim and the river was a long way down. Then the councillors cried: 'Why aren't you mending it?'

'I can't,' answered the crane driver. 'I can only mend fly-wheels, not electricity. Lektro's the one for that.'

Lektro was strolling along the river bank whistling 'Loch Lomond'. The town councillors shouted: 'Lektro, climb up this minute and mend the connection.' But Lektro shouted back: 'I used to deliver nine hundred and fifty parcels with my twelve trailers and now I've been sacked.'

Then the councillors shouted: 'You're not sacked.' So Lektro climbed up and joined the crane driver. They bent over the engine together, sucked peppermints and enjoyed themselves. Then the crane driver pushed the lever back into the right position and swung the town councillors safely down on to the far shore.

When they were on firm ground again, the town councillors blushed and felt relieved and laughed and said: 'Hey! That was fun, wasn't it?' And because just then the crane driver and Lektro were both whistling 'Loch Lomond' in harmony, they also whistled 'Loch Lomond' and they waved their hats, the sun shone and the birds sang. It was a very beautiful Sunday.

But another adventure was on its way.

It was a dark summer night. Everything was so still that one could hear the fishes swimming to and fro in the river. The crane driver slept on the crane. The night-watchman sat on a truck full of silver ore and kept watch.

This is only a scouting party. Nobody else has arrived yet.

But no one came. He got very tired from keeping watch and was nodding off. How was he to know that two men were lurking behind the truck? And when he propped his head on his hands and yawned, they leapt on to the truck like cats and knocked him out before he could utter a sound. They tied him up, stuffed a dirty handkerchief into his mouth, pushed him into an empty margarine barrel and nailed down the lid.

They then went down to the river bank and called: 'Tu-whit-tu-whoo!' three times, as if they were owls. A boat came out of the darkness and tied up next to the crane. Six other men carefully slid the anchor into the water and leapt ashore. Now there were eight men altogether. They were all barefooted and they crept up to the crane, banged on the girders and shouted: 'Oy! Wake up! Start loading!' The crane driver rubbed his eyes and called out: 'It's not seven o'clock yet. Where's the nightwatchman?'

They replied: 'He's gone fishing by the river.' And added: 'You're to load the silver ore into that boat. It's a rush job.' The crane driver asked: 'Who sent you?' And the men replied:

'The town clerk. It's the emperor of Japan's birthday tomorrow and we're to cast a statue of the Madonna out of the ore for him. Get a move on,' they said, 'we'll give you a hundred pounds if you do. Then you can buy yourself a motor-bike.'

The crane driver called down: 'It's only two o'clock in the morning. I've never done any loading at two o'clock before.'

The men said: 'That's right, two o'clock in the morning. We haven't much time. Get a move on.'

So the crane driver said: 'All right.' He rolled up his sleeves, switched on the engine and sounded the siren as he did every morning. When the siren started to howl, the men were furious and shouted: 'Turn that thing off, you half-wit.' But the siren made such a noise the crane driver could not hear a word. So when it had finished howling, the men called: 'Look down here!'

The crane driver answered: 'Can't see a thing.' The men yelled: 'Switch a torch on, then.' And when the crane driver shone his torch down he saw that the eight men were wearing red handkerchiefs on their heads and black and white striped shirts and that each one of them was holding a double-barrelled pistol in his hand. They were all aiming at his heart.

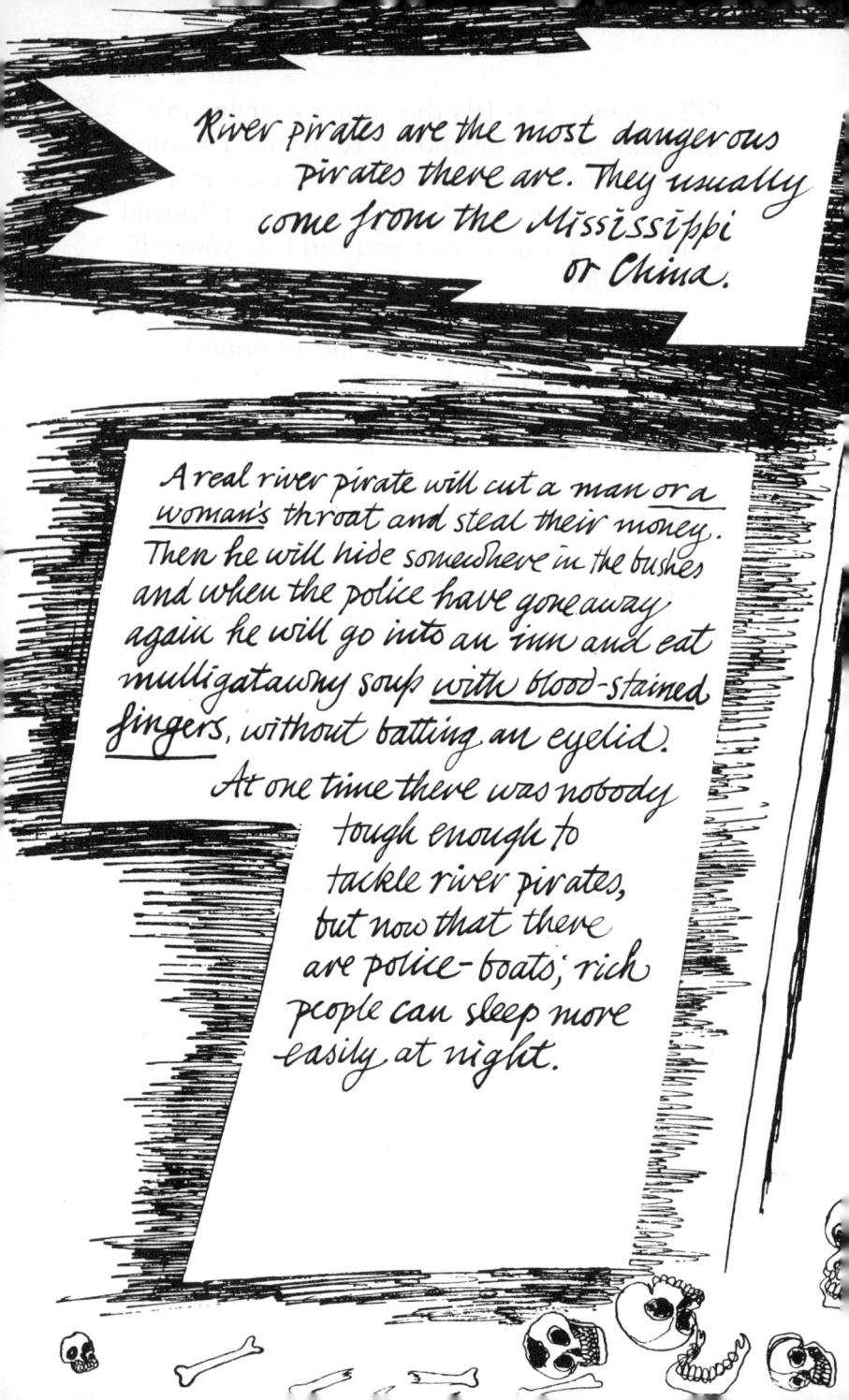

River pirates are the most dangerous pirates there are. They usually come from the Mississippi or China.

A real river pirate will cut a man or a woman's throat and steal their money. Then he will hide somewhere in the bushes and when the police have gone away again he will go into an inn and eat mulligatawny soup _with blood-stained fingers_, without batting an eyelid.

At one time there was nobody tough enough to tackle river pirates, but now that there are police-boats, rich people can sleep more easily at night.

They yelled: 'And now make it snappy, you good-for-nothing, if you value your life!' And one of them shot the torch out of his hand and laughed: 'Ho ho ho!' The crane driver had a lump in his throat and got gooseflesh all over, for he had read about the river pirates and especially about Big Burton when he was still a boy at school—Big Burton, known as the most savage pirate captain of them all, who always laughed 'ho ho ho' three times while carrying out each robbery.

The crane driver sat down at the controls and loaded the silver ore from the truck into the pirates' ship. He was not very easy in his mind as every now and then the pirates would send a bullet past his ears. 'Just a friendly warning,' they would shout. 'Get on with it.' In the distance the sound of police cars could already be heard. The police had set out the moment they had heard the siren go off in the middle of the night.

The crane driver was just picking up the last of the silver ore out of the truck, when the river pirates jumped on board their ship and aimed their pistols at his heart. The police cars were already quite near and if the crane driver were dead, nobody would know which direction the pirates had taken. The crane driver trembled with fright and in his terror he let go of the

lever when the grab was high above the ground.
The grab opened and the heavy lumps of ore fell
down on to the ship. Four pirates were killed
and the ship rocked so hard that the others
could not aim properly. Their shots went wide.
The crane driver seized the screw of the ship
with his grab, tore it off and let it fall on to the
helm. Now the helmsman was dead, too. When
the other pirates ran to plug up the hole where
the screw had been, the crane driver picked up
all three of them in the grab and dipped them
into the water. Their pistols got damp and they
could not shoot any more and when the police
cars drove up, the crane driver said: 'Here you
are, the last three.'

The police locked up the river pirates in their Black Maria and felt very proud. The police sergeant was immediately promoted to the rank of inspector. (The night-watchman was rescued from the margarine barrel after they had heard him shout in a muffled way, and from then on, every November, he had an attack of lumbago.)

The news of the crane driver's heroic deed spread through the country like wildfire. At three o'clock in the morning the police knew about it. By four o'clock all the lamplighters knew about it and told the road sweepers. The road sweepers wrote the news on the bridges

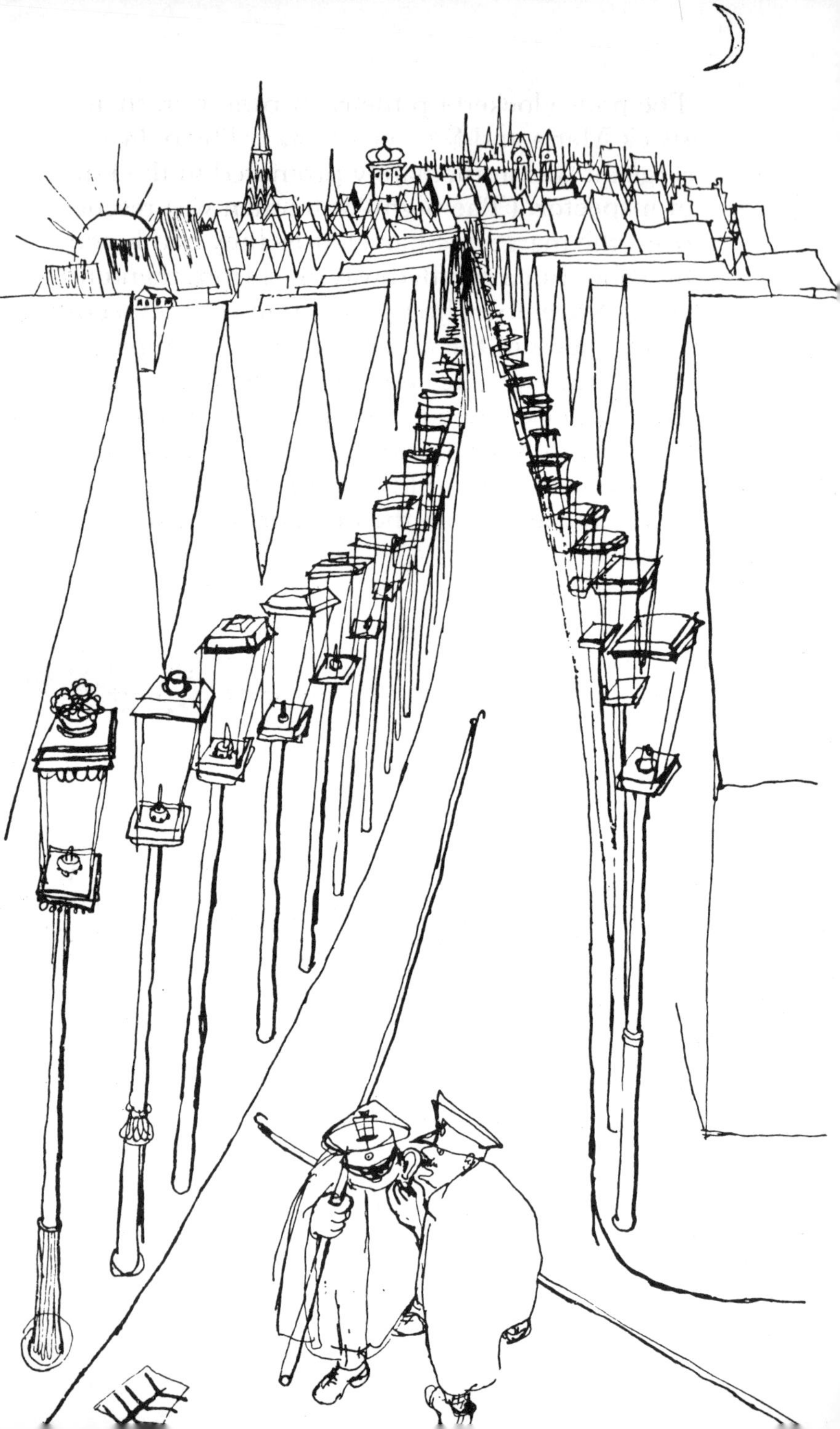

where the milk women read it. And as soon as the milk women knew it, the whole town did, too. Everywhere there was great rejoicing. The townsfolk gathered round the crane. The state schools were given a holiday. Lektro had nothing but punctures all day long, and in every pub they played 'Loch Lomond'. And in the evening along came the town clerk, the mayor and the twelve town councillors, all wearing dark suits, and they presented a medal to the crane driver. It was the famous pirate medal, gilded and with a green stone set in it. He got a rise in pay, too.

Lektro bought the crane driver some brown swimming trunks with a gold stripe. He felt they matched the new medal better. The man with the ox team gave him a permanent wave and when the crane driver sunbathed on Sundays, the girls from the bakery could see the

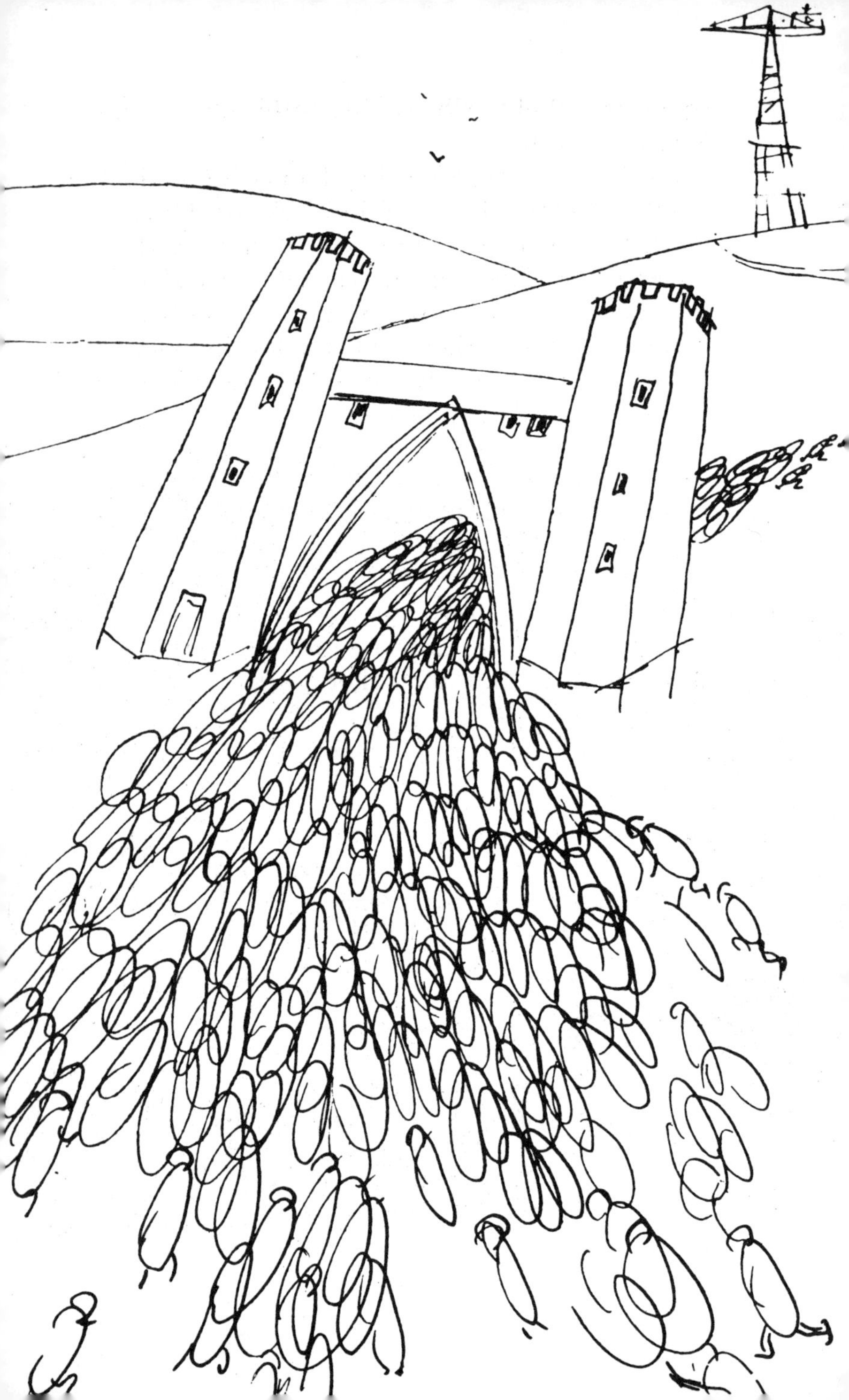

pirate medal glittering on his heroic chest from a long way off.

As the sun rose, after they had celebrated all night, the crane driver said to Lektro: 'How many bottles have we finished?' Lektro said: 'Seventeen!' The crane driver said: 'I feel as if all that business with the pirates were only a dream.' Lektro replied: 'That's not the point. An adventure is an adventure.' So they decided that it had really happened.

Winter came—summer came—winter returned, followed once more by summer; and life was always the same.

Whatever the season, there were coals to load, crates to load; crates to load, coals to load.

But it was always fun, for summer was warm and bright and Lektro daydreamed; in winter, hoar-frost lay on the crane and, when the breeze blew from the town, the iron hummed high and clear like crystal, while the coal looked so black that the ravens were jealous.

Lektro brought the daily paper to the crane driver every day and would stay just long enough to suck a peppermint. On Sunday mornings the town councillors came to be ferried across, for there was still no bridge. The girls from the bakery married young butchers and plumbers, but by then their younger sisters had grown up and it was they who now laughed up at the crane driver.

There was no better crane driver in the whole country than the man in the blue cap who wore the pirate medal. The crane was a giant with an iron arm and the man was its heart. When he had a twinge in the little toe of his left foot, he knew that a grain of sand had got stuck in the cog wheels. He would then take the engine to bits and would not rest until the grain of sand was found. When his right ear itched, he would realize that a screw had worked loose somewhere. He would climb all over the iron structure with his screwdriver and when the lorry drivers called out: 'Oy! We want to start loading!' He would call down: 'Hang on a moment, there's a screw loose,' and he would go on looking for it until it was found and tightened up again and then his ear would stop itching too.

One day, however, Lektro drove up in great excitement.

'Prices are going up,' he shouted. 'They're all hoarding. Got any money saved?'

The crane driver shouted down: 'Hundred and seventy-three pounds.'

Lektro shouted: 'Chuck it down and I'll get you some things. What do you want?'

The crane driver yelled: 'Peppermints and shaving soap and a new flint for my lighter! And two new torch batteries!'

'Don't be daft,' called Lektro. 'You want to get essentials.'

'What's essential?' asked the crane driver.

'Flour and salt,' called Lektro enthusiastically. 'Flour and salt are very essential. Nearly everyone's buying them.'

Rrrr whee—off he went.

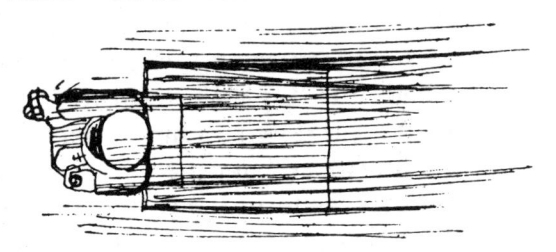

In the evening Lektro drove up again. He brought a trailer filled with sacks of flour and bags of peppermints, a carton of torch batteries and twelve pairs of long underpants and an old trumpet. The crane driver's cabin was now so full of essentials that he could hardly move and whenever it rained during the night he had to sleep standing up.

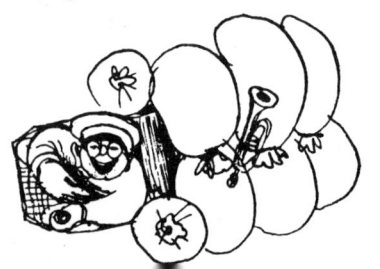

And then the crates began to weigh more and more till they were as heavy as millstones.

The crane driver gave the night-watchman twenty peppermints and asked him very quietly to have a look at what was inside the crates.

The night-watchman opened one crate and whispered: 'Nothing but iron.'

More and more ravens appeared in the country. They flew past the crane every evening at dusk and their eyes were wicked.

That autumn, on the day when frost covered the fields for the first time, the crane driver sounded his siren and noticed that there was nobody down below. There were no lorry drivers and there were no ships on the river either. The countryside was cold and empty, but the trees were full of laughing ravens.

Lektro arrived at half-past ten. He called up: 'Better come down. There's a war on.'

The crane driver asked: 'Why?'

'No idea,' Lektro answered.

'Who's the enemy?' asked the crane driver.

Lektro replied: 'The others.'

'Have you seen them?'

'No.'

'Then I'll stay up here.'

Lektro came back the next day. He arrived on foot, wearing a uniform and he called up: 'Look at my uniform. Only rayon, but it can't be helped.' And they sucked a peppermint together.

For some days the crane was deserted. Occasionally the crane driver would see soldiers marching in the distance and he heard them singing 'Loch Lomond'.

One Saturday evening the soldiers all came to the river. Lektro was there and so were the lamplighters, the road sweepers and the man with the ox team. They made fires of dry branches and warmed themselves as they drank beer and spirits. They sang and beat their drums and enjoyed themselves. The ravens were present too. They blinked because the fire dazzled them and they opened their beaks, but no sound came out.

'Hi, Lektro! What about those ravens?' the crane driver shouted his loudest, but he could not even hear his own voice. He kicked against the girders, whistled through his fingers and he yelled: 'Hoy! Hoy!' But the air lay heavily on the land and muffled all sound. And along the river bank came Death, riding on a pale horse.

He rode past the soldiers, looking at each one, and the crane driver shouted even more desperately: 'Lektro!' But the soldiers heard nothing and they did not see the pale horse with Death as the rider. When, in desperation, the crane driver threw down tins and screws to attract their attention, nobody noticed them. And the crane driver returned to his cabin and felt very sad.
  Next morning the enemy arrived.
  Both sides loaded their guns. Bullets whistled across the waves, the earth was burnt and by midday men were lying on their backs dying from their wounds. They were young, they had a motorbike at home, or a garden, some of them belonged to a swimming club and they would have liked to stay alive. Lektro was one of them. He looked over at the crane and the crane driver could see that he was daydreaming.

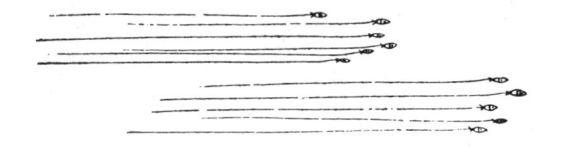

He wanted to climb down and give his friend a peppermint, but it was not possible because the enemy were shooting at the crane. Lektro once more said very quietly: 'I've got a puncture.'

Planes arrived. They looked like silver fish. They flew very high and when they were over the town, Death on the pale horse appeared. Then houses and churches exploded and crashed into the streets and the air was so hot that trees withered and the black smoke suffocated the ravens.

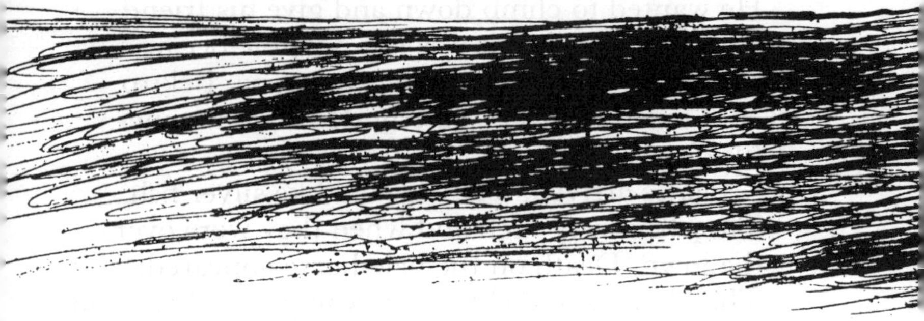

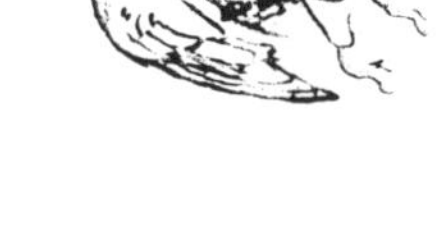

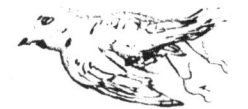

Then the country was sad
and the earth wept.

When the fire died down and the black smoke had been blown away by the wind, the survivors crawled out of their cellars and warmed themselves by the hot stones, for winter had arrived. The weather got still colder and the crane driver saw the people leave the ruined city and move into another country.

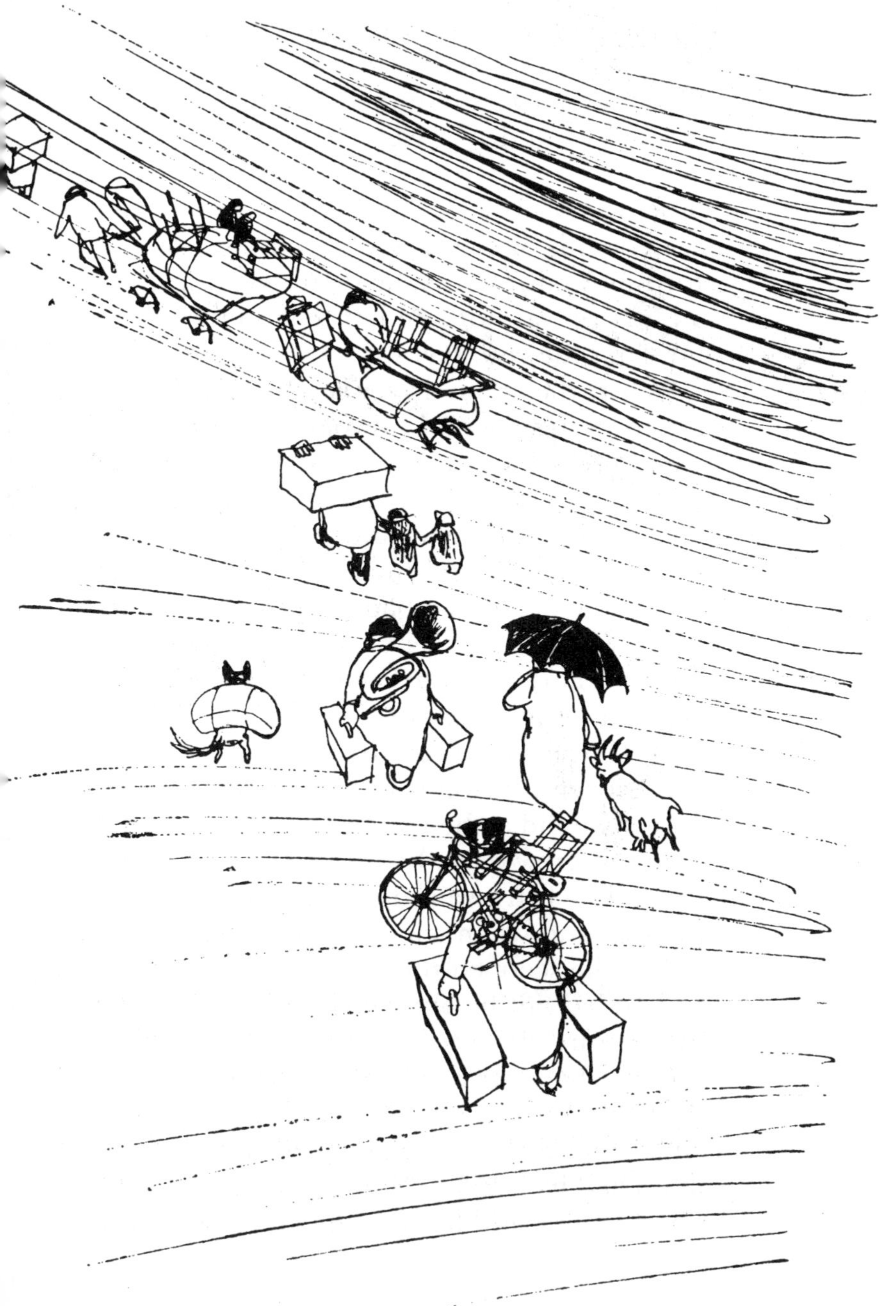

In the deserted city dogs and cats howled in the moonlight and when the great winds blew the crane girders hummed sadly.

Crane and driver were alone.

The sea covered the land. The crane driver had seen clouds of green smoke coming from behind the mountain. Then the dams were destroyed and there was nothing left to stop the sea from flooding the country.

When the crane driver sounded his siren in the morning, he noticed that the crane was standing in the sea. What had been town, river and fields was now a vast expanse of salty water.

But what difference did that make? He was the crane driver and the crane was in working order. He had seven bags full of mints and the cabin was full of essentials. He sat down at the controls and began to scoop the sea water on his right into the sea on his left and the sea water on his left into the sea on his right. He did this from seven till twelve and from one until five and as he did so he whistled 'Loch Lomond'. When it grew dark, he hung a lantern on the grab. The fish swam up to see what was happening, and when enough had collected down below, he scooped them up with the grab. When he needed salt he climbed down and scraped it off the girders. And he set a cask under the gutter whenever it rained. So he had fresh water to drink and use for cooking. He baked himself small round loaves and he served up boiled fish and fried fish. Every Sunday he went for a walk on the crane and let the sun shine on him. He

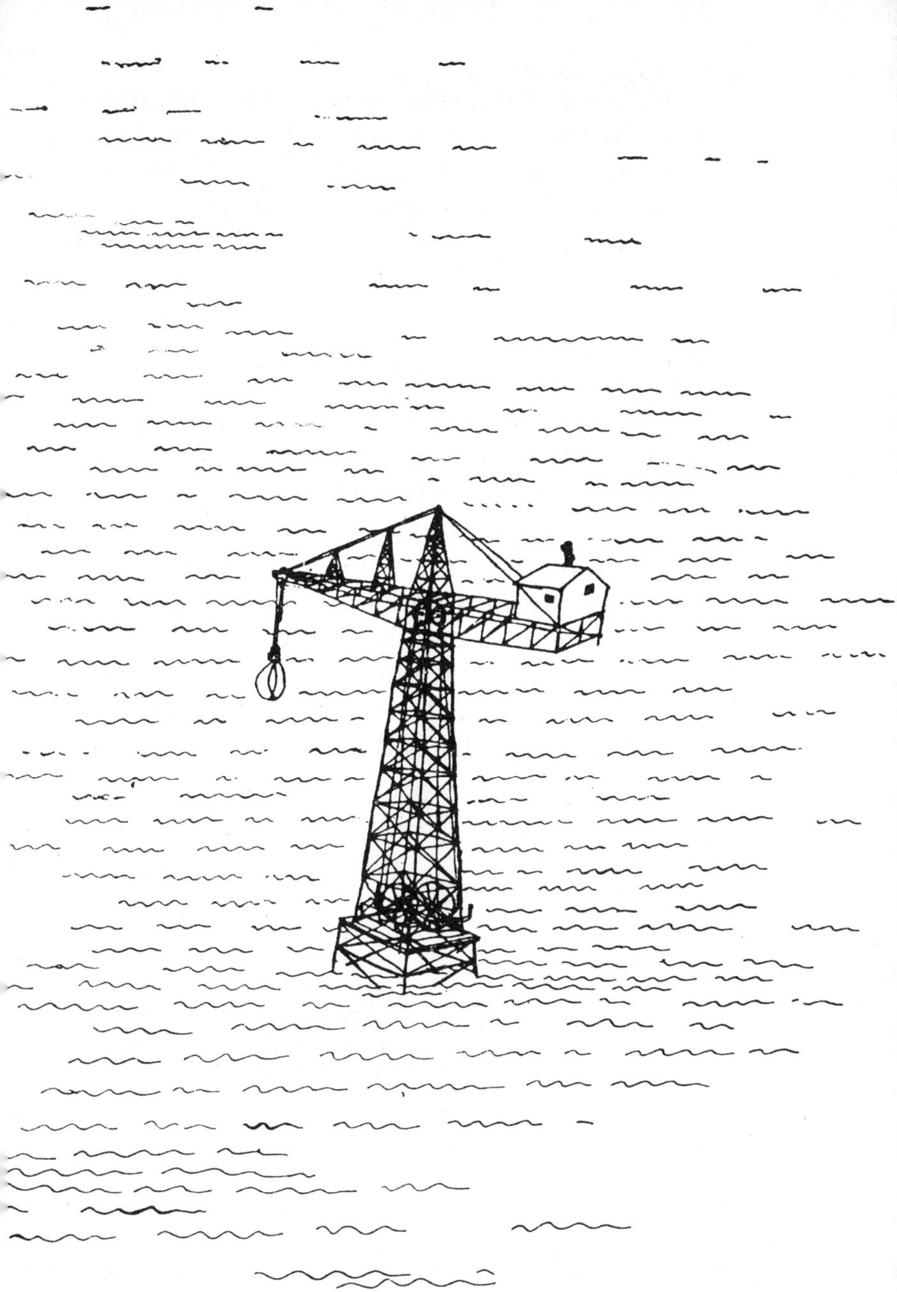

wore his pirate medal on his chest and knew that the sea monsters and mermaids could see him and that they were thinking: 'There's the crane driver. He caught an elephant and he disposed of eight pirates in one night. What a man!'

At the end of four weeks the last drop of petrol had been used up. The engine sputtered a last ft-ft and fell silent. The crane stood still. And that evening, when the crane driver wanted to fry some fish, he saw that there was no more wood left to make a fire. He lay down and wondered what to do about it. Next morning he began to unpick one of the pairs of long pants and twist the yarn into a fishing line. When the line was long enough, he stretched it between two iron bars and rubbed it with wax so that it would be stronger. He then made a hook from a piece of bent wire and kept a look-out for big fishes.

(Seen from the fishes' point of view.)

Within three days he had caught four big fishes.
He cut them open and squeezed them until he
had collected half a pail full of fish-oil.

From then on he cooked his fish over an oil
flame and when it grew dark he lit an oil lamp.

One day, when he climbed down to scrape off
some salt, he noticed that the ironwork above
water level was getting rusty. That was dangerous. 'It's the damp air,' he thought. 'It's so
damp, it's rusting the ironwork.' He climbed up
again, went into the cabin and said out loud:
'The crane's going rusty.'

He then climbed down again and scraped the
rust off with his knife and when the iron was
bright again, he spread oil on it. It took him a
long time to scrape all the rust off the ironwork
and by the time he had reached the top of the
crane, the damp wind had blown the oil off the
lower part and he had to start all over again.

The sea creatures watched him as he climbed all
over the iron structure, scraping off rust, day
after day, from seven until midday and from one
o'clock till five.

Every evening he lay in wait for the big fishes.

Night followed day and day followed night.
In summer the wind blew from the east and in
winter from the west. At night, when sharks

bumped into the iron structure, the crane would shake gently. But sometimes the sky grew dark and the sea was stirred up by storms. Waves as high as houses battered against the crane, water hissed and sprayed up to the top and the girders creaked and strained—but none of the screws worked loose and the crane stood fast.

One night, however, as the crane driver was going to bed, he heard something in the distance. He climbed to the top of the crane and looked out across the ocean but could see nothing. He put his hand to his ear and listened.

Then he said to himself: 'Ships! I'll bet they're ships.'

Well, he was the crane driver and those ships were none of his business. But then he cried:

'Good lord! How can they find their way in the dark?'

From then on the sea creatures saw the crane driver stand outside his cabin with a torch every night. He would whistle 'Loch Lomond' and after each verse he would switch his torch on and off three times and shout: 'Ahoy there! This is a lighthouse! Ahoy there!'

When the last torch battery had been used, he took up his oil lamp. He would pass it three times in front and three times behind him, once with his right hand and once with his left, so that he did not tire too quickly. One Sunday he wrote on a piece of paper:

<u>LETTER</u>
TO THE SHIPS:
THIS IS TO LET YOU KNOW THAT I HAVE <u>NO MORE BATTERIES</u> BUT I AM SIGNALLING WITH MY <u>OIL LAMP</u> AND I WONDERED WHETHER YOU COULD SEND ME SOME <u>NEW</u> BATTERIES PLEASE.
THE CRANE DRIVER

He slipped the letter into a bottle and waited until it was autumn and the wind blew the waves over towards the ships. He then threw the bottle into the sea.

He was the crane driver and very reliable. He scraped off rust and fished and signalled from dawn till dusk, from dusk until dawn. He had no time to sleep and he had no time to feel lonely.

Once the waves brought him a small piece of wood. It was no larger than a hand, but the crane driver was pleased because he had not seen any wood for a long time. December came. On Christmas Eve, while he waved his lantern, he sang 'Silent Night' in addition to 'Loch Lomond' as well and as loudly as he could for the ships and for the sea creatures. The sea was calm. The stars twinkled and the wind took up the song, turned it into gleaming ice-pearls and carried it gently out into the night, across the sea and far behind the mountain.

The crane driver went into the cabin and set
fire to the wood. He warmed his hands and face
at the flame and then he cupped his hands over
the embers and blew into them. The sparks flew
up, pricking against his fingers and face and a
red glow ran along the wall and beyond the wall
his world came to an end. A ship appeared, as
big as a town. It was white and yellow, but as it
came closer, the crane driver saw that it was
made of silver with golden chimneys. Lektro
stood on the bridge, steering the ship towards
the crane. The girls from the bakery leaned from
the portholes waving white flowers while on
deck the river pirates flourished red lanterns
and threw knives. But the knives turned into
many-coloured birds which fluttered round the
ship. Lektro then climbed up the crane and sat

down beside the crane driver. He was a king.
He had a crown on his head and wore a coat
made of precious stones and the crane driver
noticed that his own overalls were made of blue
jewels. Next to Lektro sat the silver lion. Blue
smoke billowed round the ship and all the sea
creatures came out of the water. They were
brown and black and curious and Lektro sucked
a peppermint, but he looked neither to right nor
left. He raised his hand and the ship spread out
over the sea and turned into a town. The crane
stood in the middle and the iron girders were
golden now. The town councillors sat in houses
drinking beer and spirits and enjoying themselves and there were lions and bears in the
streets, but they were tame. A call came from
below. The crane driver said to Lektro: 'Someone's calling.' But Lektro had disappeared. The
crane driver exclaimed: 'It's only a dream!
Nothing's real!' But there was Lektro and it was
all real once more. The crane driver heard the
cry again, Lektro disappeared and blue smoke
lay over the town. Everything grew dark and
again the crane driver heard the cry. It was a
mournful cry. The crane driver left his cabin
and touched the girders. They were made of
cold, hard iron. There was not the smallest
trace of gold. He took the oil lamp and climbed
down. An eagle sat on the lowest girder and he
was unhappy.

'What's wrong?' asked the crane driver.

'I can't fly any more,' said the eagle.

And the crane driver noticed that the eagle
had broken a wing. He tucked the eagle under

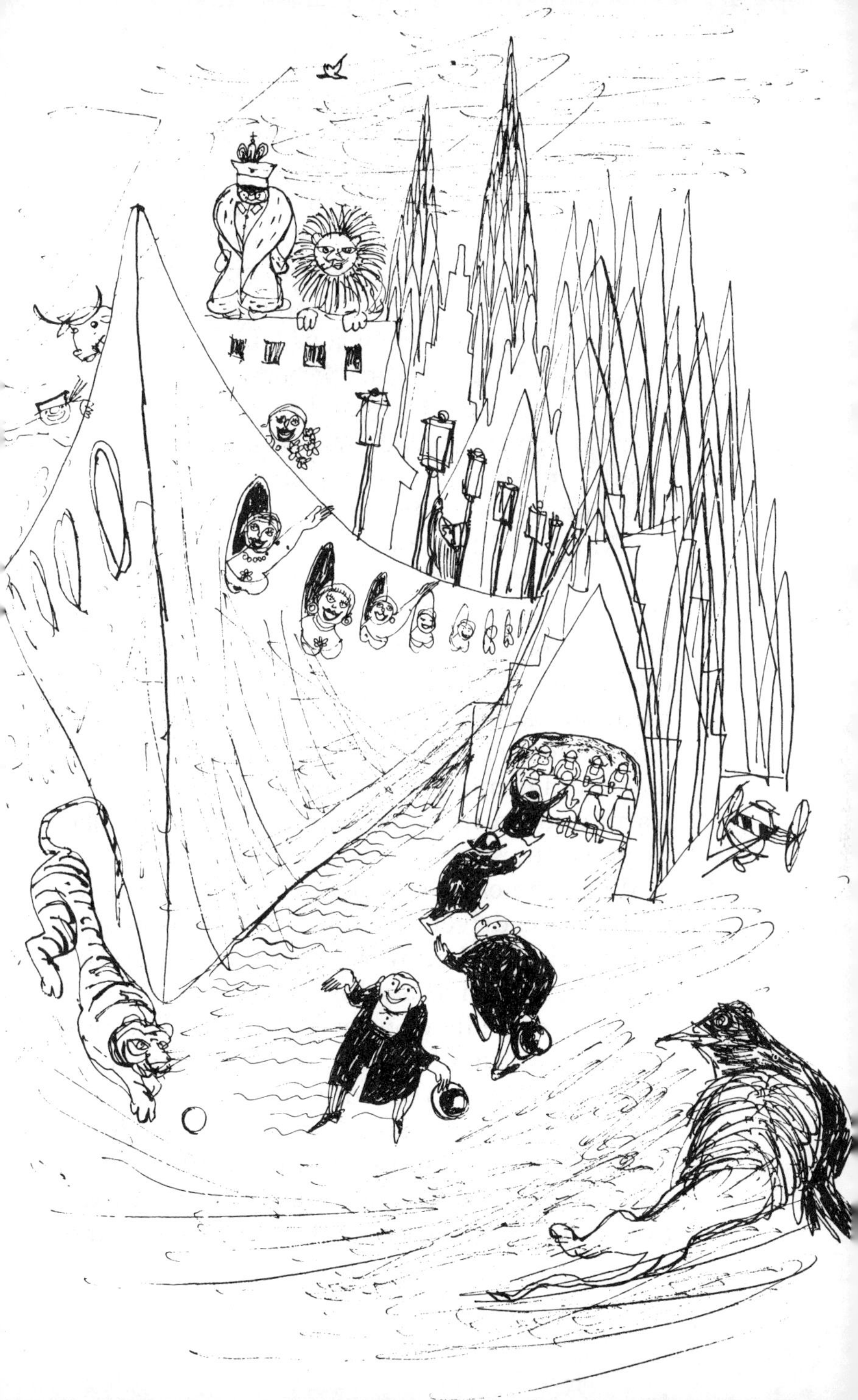

his arm and carried him carefully up to the
cabin. He made splints from fish bones and put
them on the broken wing and bandaged it with
white linen. He then gave the eagle something
to eat and drink and wrapped him in a pair of
warm underpants. And when he went out again
to signal the ships, the eagle went to sleep.

When the eagle's wing had mended, he said
to the crane driver: 'You needn't go fishing any
more. I'll take that over. What do you like best?'

The crane driver said: 'Cod.'

So the eagle flew out over the sea. He cruised
in circles waiting for a codfish to venture to the
surface. And when one did, he plunged down
like an arrow and seized it in his talons. He flew
back to the crane and said to the crane driver:
'Here you are. Cod.' The crane driver was surprised and very pleased indeed. But sometimes

the eagle did not see any fish however hard he looked—and no one has sharper eyes than an eagle. 'There must be a shark nearby,' said the crane driver. 'Nothing comes to the surface when there are sharks about. Curse them!' And whenever a shark surfaced near the crane, the crane driver would say to the eagle: 'Go on, let him have it!' And the eagle would plummet down on to the shark screaming: 'Buzz off!' and punch a hole in the shark's back with his beak. Before the shark could lash out at him with its tail, the eagle was up and away. Afterwards the crane driver and the eagle would sit outside the cabin sucking a peppermint and feeling happy.

So it soon happened that in the part of sea surrounding the crane most of the sharks had holes in their backs. But there's no need to feel sorry for them. They are the worst crooks in the ocean. Possibly they are even worse than the river pirates.

One Sunday, when they went for a walk on the crane, the crane driver said to the eagle: 'You are now my best friend, so this evening I'll tell you my secret. Can you keep a secret?'

'All eagles can keep secrets,' said the eagle. Then they sat down on an iron girder and waited for night to fall.

Even before the moon had risen, when it was still pitch-dark, the crane driver went into the cabin with the eagle and locked all the doors and windows. He went very close to the eagle and whispered so quietly that only an eagle could have heard him: 'It works.'

And he pointed at the engine and the crane. 'Everything's oiled, everything's in order,' he whispered. 'Do you know, if I had some petrol

I could turn it in all directions.' He paused. 'That's my secret.'

The eagle nodded and was very proud that no one, apart from the crane driver and himself, knew the secret.

In the spring the eagle noticed a bottle bobbing about in the ocean and brought it to the crane driver. It was the same bottle which the crane driver had sent to the ships long ago, but there was a different message inside. The crane driver was delighted. He tweaked the eagle's feathers, whistled 'Loch Lomond' and exclaimed: 'We've had a letter! We've had a letter!'

The letter said:

I haven't got any torch batteries. I have a potato field. Have you got a boat?

The crane driver read the letter to the eagle six times, then he said: 'So we've got a friend. He lives far behind the mountain on an island. And he's got a potato field. He must be quite old. His writing's old-fashioned.'

The eagle wanted to fly there right away, but not even an eagle can fly that far. His wings get tired and he falls into the sea and there is the risk that sharks might eat him. So the crane driver immediately wrote a letter back:

NO I HAVEN'T. I AM THE CRANE DRIVER. ALL DAY LONG I SCRAPE RUST OFF THE CRANE AND AT NIGHT I AM A LIGHTHOUSE TO THE SHIPS. AN EAGLE LIVES HERE WITH ME AND WE EAT NOTHING BUT FISH. CHEERIO.

When it was autumn and the wind blew from the other direction, the crane driver gave the bottle containing this letter to the eagle. The eagle flew as far as he could, but he could not reach the mountain. So he dropped the bottle into the sea and they both hoped it would reach the man with the potato field safely.

But the eagle had noticed a great crowd of sharks gathering just in front of the mountain and he said to the crane driver: 'There are about thirty of them. Maybe forty. The water was quite black down there and they all had holes in their backs.'

The crane driver looked thoughtful and scratched his ear. 'Thirty to forty sharks,' he said to the eagle. 'And all with holes in their backs? Are you sure?'

'At least thirty or forty,' said the eagle. 'Do you think they're up to something?'

The crane driver and the eagle went into the cabin and locked doors and windows. Then the crane driver said: 'I know what it is. They're gathering in front of the mountain and when there are enough of them, maybe a hundred, they'll try to knock down the crane.'

The crane driver and the eagle both went rather pale. But the crane driver said: 'They can't scare me.' The eagle said: 'Me neither.' The crane driver took a screwdriver and made sure that none of the screws was working loose. They were all in order and there was not a trace of rust on the structure. It had no flaws and was flexible. He then unscrewed a girder right at the top and took a file out of his tool box. He filed one end of the girder to a point. It took a day and a night. When the crane driver had finished, the iron point was long and sharp and fine as a needle. The eagle did the signalling and flew across the sea to keep an eye on the sharks.

'They're still in front of the mountain,' reported the eagle. 'And there are more of them arriving all the time.'

The crane driver then plaited all his fishing lines together into a strong rope and tied the rope to the end of his pointed iron girder.

'Now let 'em come,' he said. He climbed to the top of the crane and looked out across the sea, but the sharks did not appear. They were still waiting to increase their numbers and the eagle still circled over them.

On Monday the eagle flew back to the crane and when he was still quite a long way off he shouted: 'They're coming!'

The crane driver quickly did a few exercises on the crane to limber up and the eagle sharpened his beak till it was like a razor. But when they saw the large black mass in the sea coming closer and closer they crouched on the girder like two tigers waiting for their prey and tried to keep calm. The man had lashed himself to the girder and grasped his improvised harpoon in his left hand and the rope in his right. Both figures looked as if they had been turned to stone.

Once the great horde of sharks was close, the sea surged furiously and, as the sharks hurled themselves against the girders, the rest pressed after them so hard that many were cut in two. Then the sharks rammed the crane from all sides. The sea raged and foamed. The sharks dashed their heads against the crane until it swayed and quivered. The crane driver flung his harpoon into the midst of the sharks. He hurled it with such force that the point went right through several sharks. Then he hauled the harpoon up by its rope and flung it down again. Meanwhile the eagle plunged down and wrought

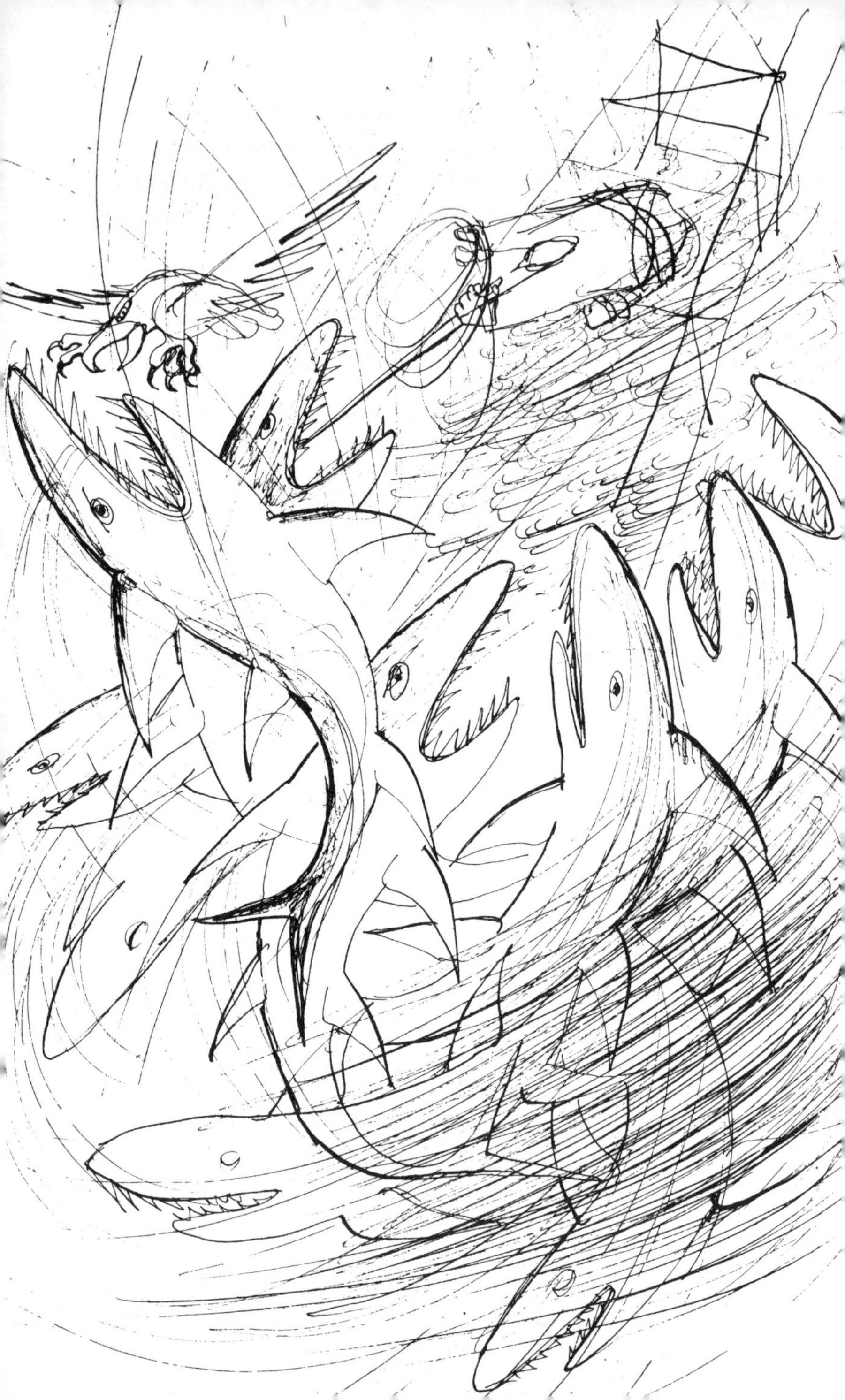

havoc among the sharks with his beak. But the
number of sharks did not seem to diminish.
They swirled and lashed, gurgled and hissed, and
after a while were able to twist one of the lower
girders. The crane strained and shook and it was
a good thing the crane driver had strapped
himself to it. Suddenly the sharks turned and
surged away, but this was not the end of the
battle. The eagle saw them gather in the distance
and confer. They charged back again in a dense
pack. This time they attacked the crane from
one side and tried to push it over by smashing
the foundations. The crane driver prayed that
they might miss the crane but they did not.
They battered into it like an avalanche. This
time the crane was shaken to its foundations, but
it remained upright. Then they tried to ram it
from another side. They never stopped attacking
and the ocean seethed like a witch's cauldron.
The sea creatures peered out from their hiding-
places and trembled with fear.

By nightfall there remained only half as many
sharks as there had been in the morning. And
the crane was still standing firm. They withdrew,
defeated.

When the sharks got back to the mountain
each blamed the other for the fact that the crane
was still standing. They became furious and the
eagle could see them attacking each other.

'What shall we have for supper?' he asked.

'Cod,' replied the crane driver.

But first they went into the cabin and leaned
against the wall. They closed their eyes and slept
like logs while the sea calmed down once more.

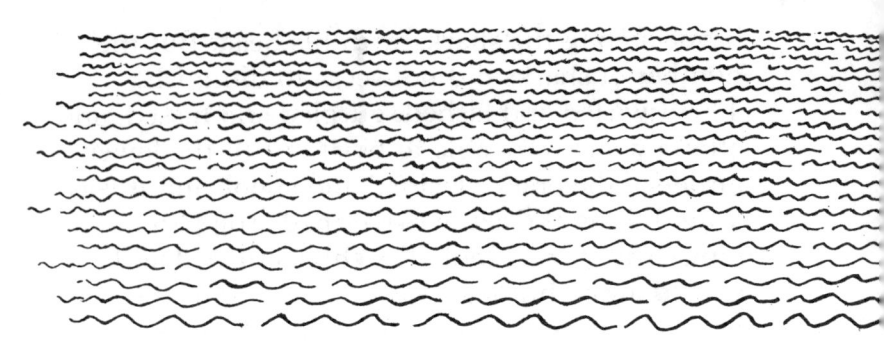

From that day there were sharks in the sea with a hole right through them so the sea-water flowed from one side to the other and little fishes were able to take a short cut through them. This pleased the crane driver and the eagle.

One day the eagle happened to find the trumpet in the cabin.

'Is it magic?' he asked the crane driver. 'In fairy tales they always are.'

'No,' replied the crane driver. 'Lektro got it for me. It's my best trumpet.'

'Can you play it?' asked the eagle. 'I do love to hear them being played.' But the crane driver could not. From that day on the sea creatures were able to see the crane driver sitting on a girder every evening playing the trumpet, while the eagle sat opposite him drawing in his head. 'Why do you always draw in your head when I play?' the crane driver asked.

'Wrong notes,' said the eagle. 'Wrong notes make eagles draw their heads in.'

'I can't hear any wrong notes,' said the crane driver. But to his surprise he noticed his own head drawing into his shoulders. However, he

You can see in this picture how mean little fishes can be.
Still, you can hardly blame them.

went on playing. He played every evening, even on Sundays. He learnt to play faster and louder and did not mind at all when the eagle drew in his head. 'Just habit,' he told himself. 'Doesn't worry me.'

But when winter came and Christmas Eve was approaching, the crane driver sent the eagle off every night to go fishing while he practised playing 'Silent Night' in the cabin. On Christmas Eve, he hid the trumpet behind his back and said to the eagle with a wink: 'What've I got behind my back?'

'No idea. An organ?'

'Nonsense,' said the crane driver. 'I'm no magician.'

'A piece of wood?' suggested the eagle.

'Nonsense,' said the crane driver. 'That was last year.'

'Well, what have you got?'

The crane driver grinned. 'A trumpet.' He winked and then laughed and because he winked, the eagle laughed too. 'And what do you think I'm going to play for you now?'

'"Loch Lomond",' said the eagle.

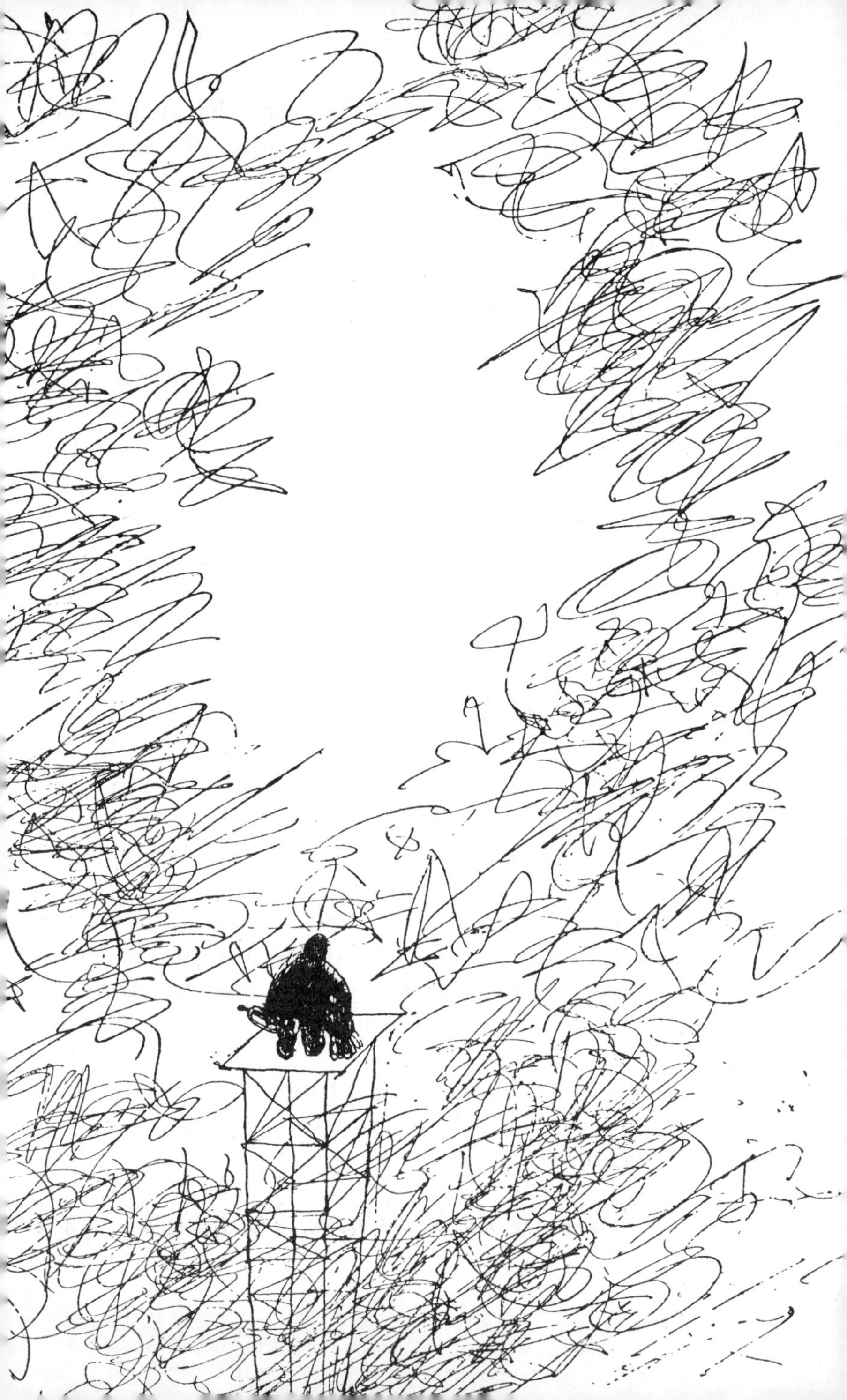

'Wrong again,' said the crane driver, pleased. 'Much better than that. I'm going to play you "Silent Night".'

The eagle leaned discreetly against a girder so that the crane driver should not notice him draw in his head and the crane driver blew into the trumpet. 'Silent Night' poured out in pure, clear tones like a church organ—at first very gently, very quietly and then growing stronger, till at last it sounded triumphantly out into the night as if there were a hundred organs. And the wind changed the song into gleaming ice-pearls and carried them far beyond the mountain and up to the stars. Then the crane driver and the eagle saw a glittering golden angel fly from star to star and both stared open-mouthed for they understood that it was a miracle. 'A hundred organs,' whispered the crane driver. And their hearts were full.

That spring there was no post for them. The crane driver got very gloomy.

'Why doesn't he write?' he complained all summer.

In the autumn he wrote another letter to the man with the potato field. He told him about the battle with the sharks and the miracle of the trumpet. He wrote it in great detail and sent it off in another bottle.

The following spring brought some post—both bottles. The man with the potato field wrote:

There are no birds here. The only things her

are sea and sand and sun, my potato field and myself. And stars at night. I have a star. The three hundred and sixtieth star on the right belongs to me. What does the trumpet look like?

In each bottle there was a potato. After the crane driver had read the letter to the eagle twelve times, he boiled the potatoes. They locked door and windows and each of them ate a potato. Then they leaned against the wall and said to each other: 'That was marvellous.'

Next autumn, when the crane driver was writing to the man with the potato field, he said to the eagle: 'How shall I describe the trumpet?'

The eagle said: 'You'll have to draw it.'

'I can't,' said the crane driver. But the eagle said: 'Have a shot.' So he did. First he tried it like the drawing on the left and then like the drawing in the middle and then like the drawing on the right. It took him days and the eagle kept saying 'That's not a real trumpet.' But at last he got it right.

This is the first trumpet the crane driver drew, but the eagle said: 'You've forgotten to show the hole at the top and the bottom.'

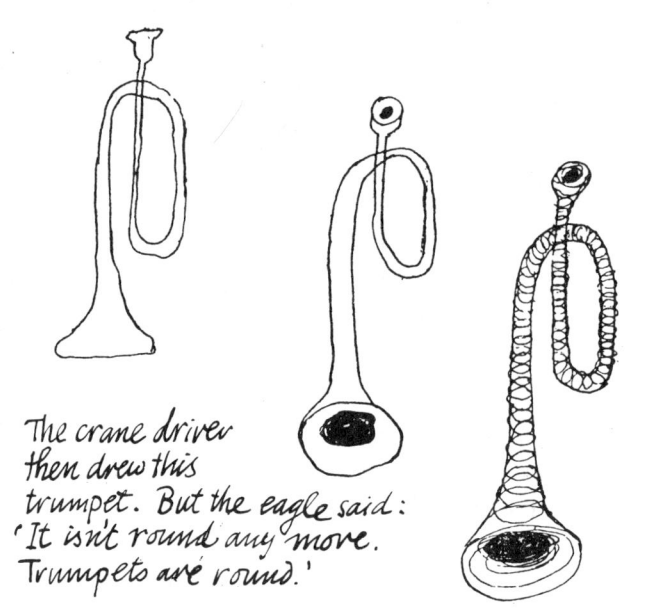

The crane driver then drew this trumpet. But the eagle said: 'It isn't round any more. Trumpets are round.'

After the crane driver had drawn it round, the eagle said: 'Well, you've drawn it round now, and there's a hole at the top and the bottom. But it still doesn't look right.'

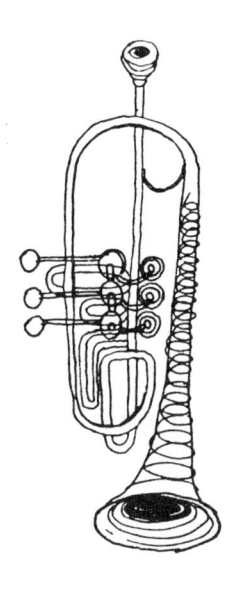

The crane driver went on trying for days. It's much harder to draw a trumpet than a bird or a rabbit (from behind).

But he got it right in the end.

That winter, the man said to the eagle: 'Why don't we choose a star, too. Do you think we could just take one?'

The eagle said: 'Of course.'

So they each chose a star and every evening they looked up at the sky expectantly, waiting for their stars to appear. But the eagle had sharper eyes than the crane driver and usually said: 'Here comes mine,' long before the crane driver could see his. And that made the crane driver cross and they were not as friendly as before.

One Sunday, the crane driver said: 'From now on we'll do things differently. A day'll be an hour; a week, a day; a month, a week; and a year'll be a month. Then we'll get letters every month.'

The eagle said: 'You can't do that. Night is night and you must show a light to the ships.'

'I'll write to the ships,' said the crane driver, 'and tell them that here on the crane each day'll be an hour, but that I'll signal for them every night.' But the eagle said: 'The sun rises every day, but my star'll come every hour and when do we sleep?'

No longer on speaking terms.

'Anything's possible,' said the crane driver.
But the eagle drew his head in and this made the crane driver furious. 'Who's the boss here, I'd like to know?' he cried. 'I am, and we could be having letters every month.' Next morning he said to the eagle: 'You've spoilt it all. I'm not speaking to you. Understand?' From that day on they ignored each other.

No longer on speaking terms.

The crane driver did his own fishing and the
eagle sat on the outermost edge of the crane
gazing into the sea and when it was cold they
both sat in the cabin but in different corners.
And when the crane driver played his trumpet,
the eagle drew in his head. They were both very
lonely and the days which had become hours
passed far more slowly than the days had done
before the crane driver changed them.
In spring, the eagle sitting on the outermost edge
of the crane, said: 'A bottle!' He only said it just
loud enough for the crane driver to hear him.
Then the crane driver climbed to the outermost
edge of the crane too and looked out over the
sea. He was very sad but he said nothing.

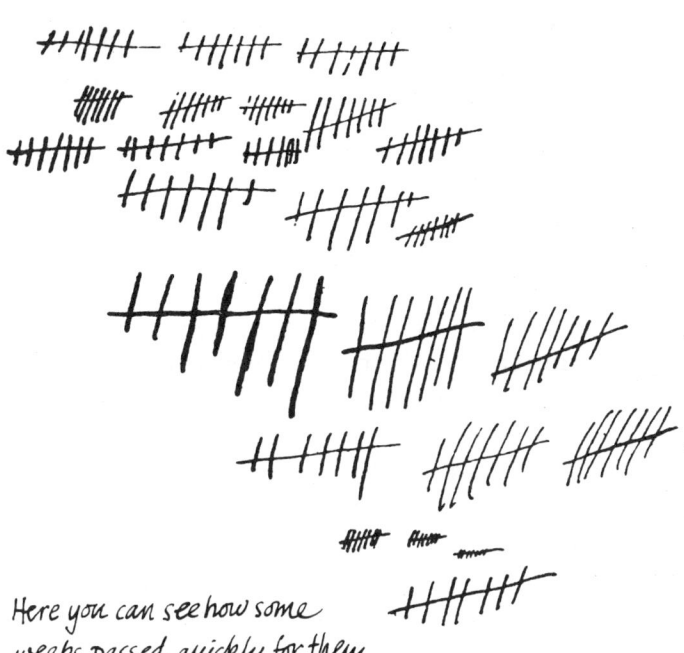

Here you can see how some weeks passed quickly for them and others seemed to take a very long time.

That night the crane driver could not sleep. Instead of scraping off the rust the next morning, he sat on the outermost edge of the crane and stared gloomily into the sea.

On the third day he said to the eagle: 'I wonder what he's written.'

The eagle said: 'The sun rises every day and a day is a day.'

The crane driver said: 'That's right.'
And the eagle flew out over the sea and fetched the bottle. They were both very happy and sucked a peppermint together. And whenever the man played the trumpet, the eagle went off and sat in the dark so that nobody could see him drawing in his head.

When another few years had gone by, the eagle noticed smoke on the horizon. He woke up the crane driver and said: 'There's smoke on the horizon.'

'That must be a ship,' said the crane driver. 'It's probably sailing behind the mountain. Go and see whether it's armed.' When the eagle came back he said: 'I didn't see any guns.'

Then the crane driver knew that the war was over and he was very happy.

Another time the eagle woke up the crane driver and said: 'There's an island near the mountain.'

The crane driver had to hold on to a girder with both hands because he was weak with joy. He nearly fell off the crane. 'You know,' he said to the eagle, 'they must be building the dams again and letting the sea drain back. Years ago this was all land. Now everything will be green again and there'll be trees and fields and flowers.' He quickly played 'Loch Lomond' on his trumpet and then they both went into the cabin. They locked door and windows and leaned against the wall dreaming of flowers, fields and trees.

The crane driver and the eagle sat on the topmost point of the crane day and night and watched the land emerge from the sea.

Finally the sea disappeared and over by the mountain things began to grow again. Soon there were only a few lakes left in the countryside, though the crane still stood in a large lake.

One evening, when the sun had passed the mountain, a stranger stood at the edge of the lake.

He was carrying a sack of potatoes over his shoulder. He waved energetically and called out: 'God be with you, God be with you.'

The crane driver waved his arms wildly in the air; then he played his trumpet and sent the eagle across the lake with some fish.

They sat looking at each other until the sun disappeared behind the mountain.

They were old friends.

When the stars came out the man from the potato field returned to his potato field.

The wind brought clouds from the mountain and during the night they sank to earth and absorbed the lakes and within sixteen Sundays the lake under the crane had disappeared and the river was back again.

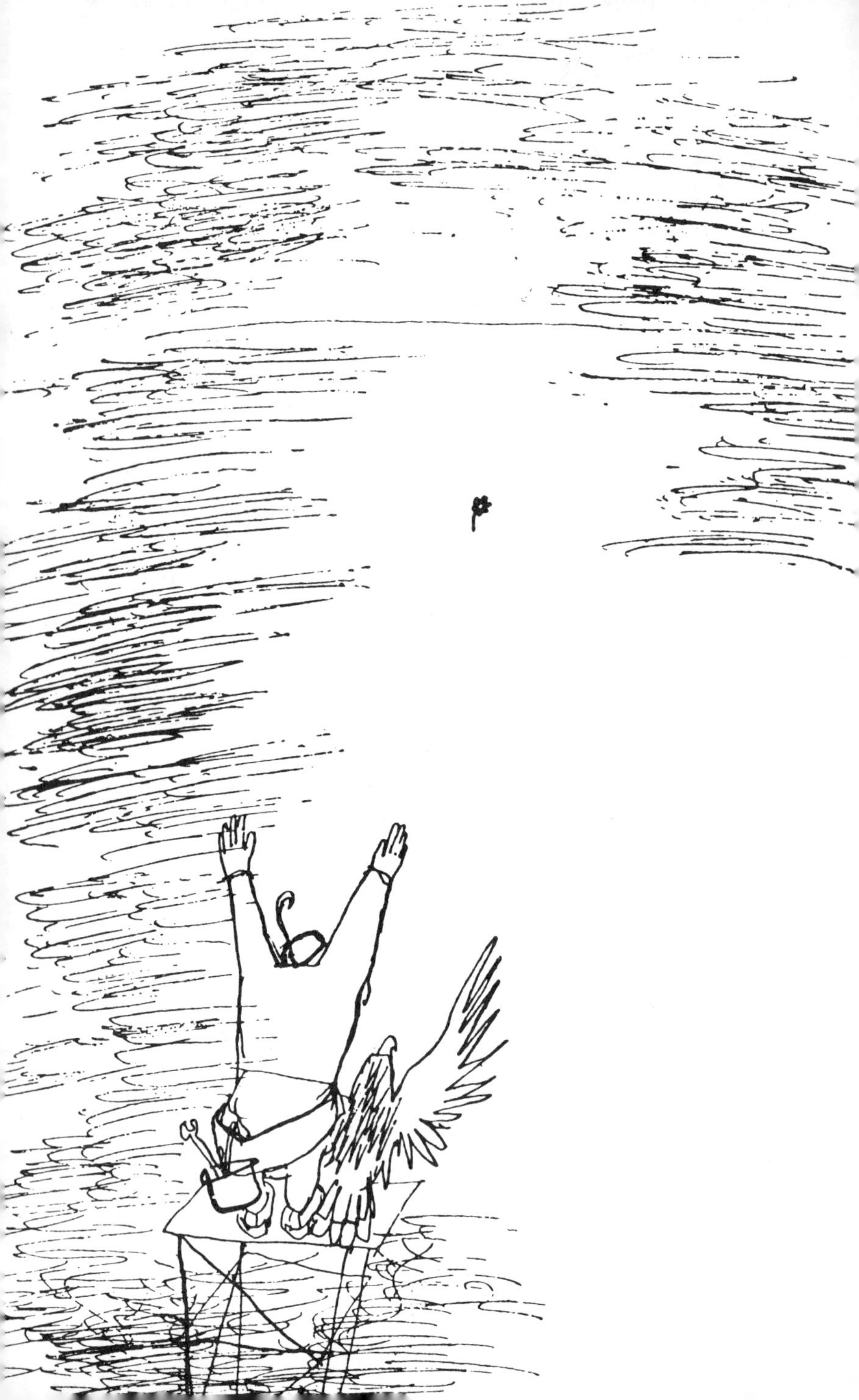

One morning a warm mist lay over the land and when the sun came and banished the mist, a single yellow flower could be seen.

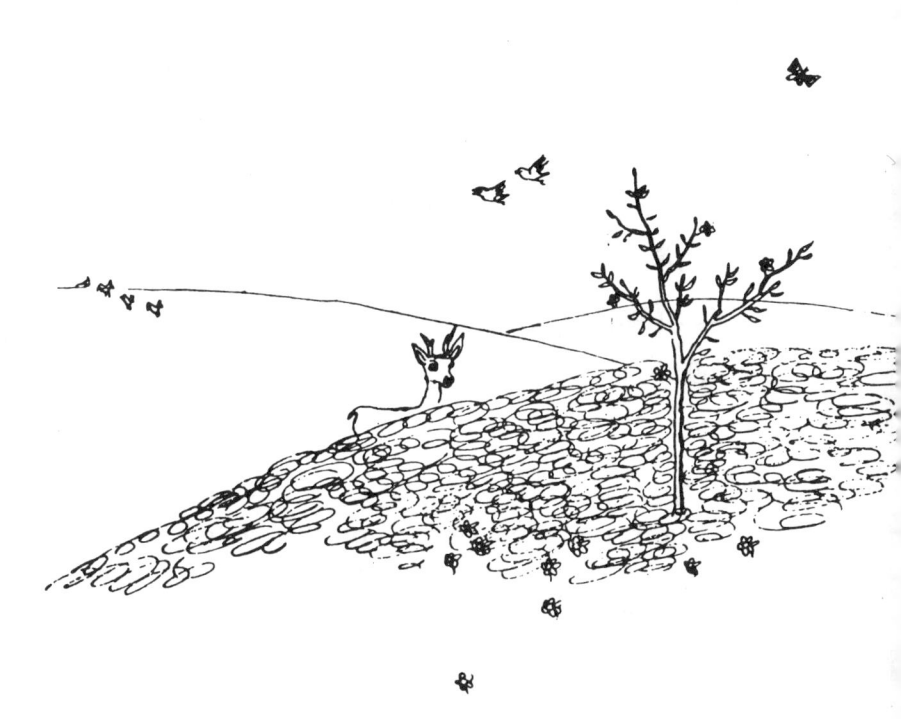

After that flowers sprang from the earth, bushes and trees grew and the crane driver and the eagle saw the animals return to the land: birds, rabbits, deer and vivid butterflies. It was spring everywhere. Foreigners came over the mountain and began to build up the town again. Farmers came and ploughed the land and sowed wheat. But they were all strangers. They were not friendly and no one came near the crane.

But a silver lion did. Every night, in the moonlight, the crane driver and the eagle saw the silver lion walk along the river looking to right and left. The crane driver said to the eagle:

'There's Lektro's silver lion. He's only a dream, anyway.'

Every day the crane driver told the eagle: 'It's still working. The crane's still working, I know it. All we need is a gallon of petrol.'

But they had no money. They each had a star, there were flowers everywhere and the river was like molten silver. It was like paradise, but they did not have any money. The eagle said: 'Let's consult the silver lion. He's probably very wise.'

That evening they sat on the lowest girder and waited for the silver lion. They each carried a flower. When the silver lion appeared they both said: 'How are you?'

The silver lion looked at them calmly. 'What's the matter with him?' asked the crane driver. The eagle said: 'He wants a song.'

'I know "Loch Lomond" and "Silent Night",' said the crane driver quickly. The silver lion shook his head. Then the eagle said: 'We need petrol, but we have no money. What should we do?' The silver lion pointed downwards. Then he went on his way.

'He means we're to look,' said the eagle.

'You can't find money by looking for it,' said the crane driver. 'It has to be earned.'

But the eagle said: 'One sometimes finds a penny.'

The eagle flew out every day, but he rarely found even a penny.

The foreigners did not drop money in the streets or in the fields. Only on market days did the eagle occasionally find a few pennies.

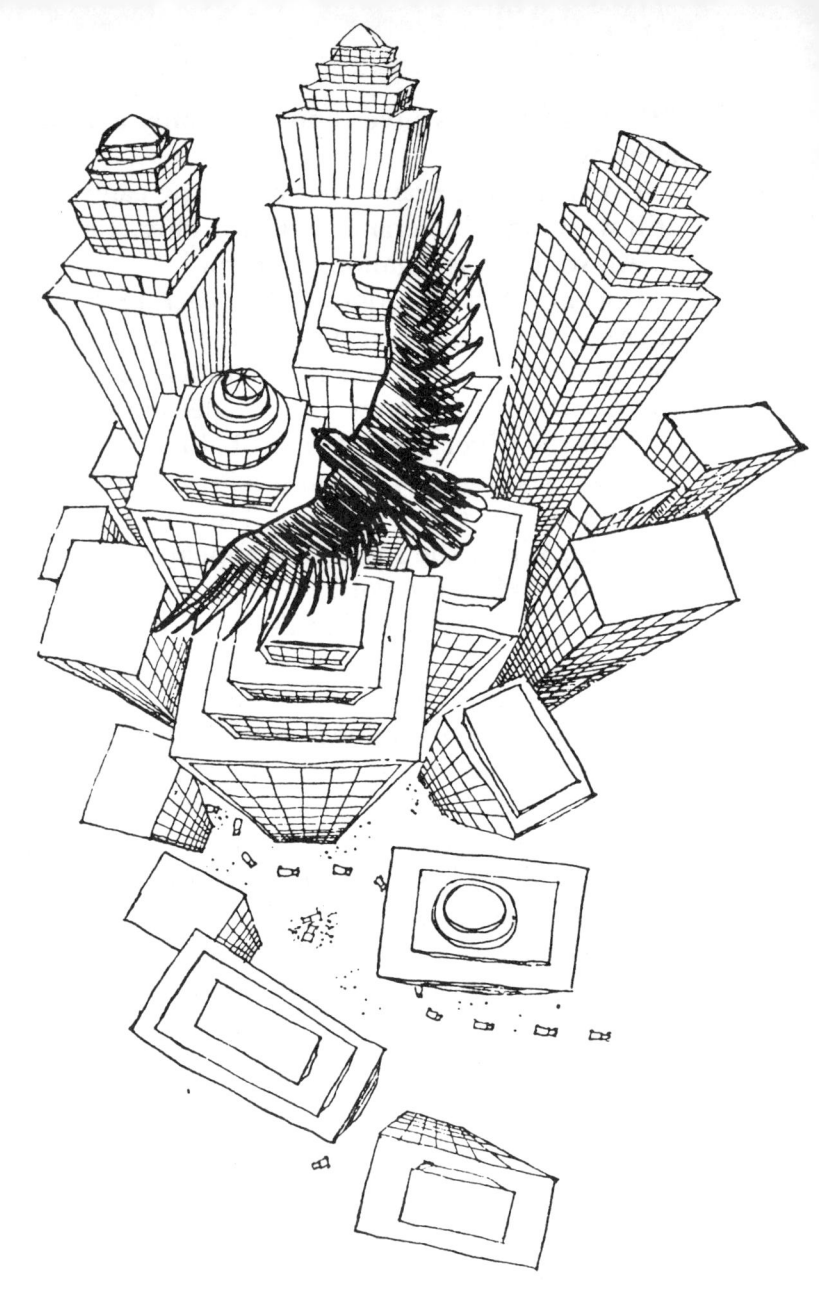

How can an eagle be expected to find anything there?

A gallon of petrol cost eighty pennies. It took them three years to collect eighty pennies. The eagle flew to a petrol station and said: 'Here are eighty pennies. A gallon of petrol, please.'

The man at the petrol station laughed and said: 'Eighty pennies—that was three years ago. Everything's gone up since then. Today petrol costs two hundred and forty pennies.'

That evening they waited for the silver lion again.

'How are you?' they said when, at midnight, he came along the river. The silver lion looked at them calmly.

The crane driver said: 'Everything's gone up. A gallon of petrol costs two hundred and forty pennies today and we've only got eighty. What shall we do?'

The silver lion went down to the river and dipped his paws in the water. Then he continued on his way along the river. When he was out of sight they noticed that each drop of water which had fallen from his paws had turned into real silver. The eagle gathered the drops up and they had a whole bag full of silver.

The man at the petrol station gaped at the eagle when he was paid in silver. He bowed five times and said: 'At your service, Mr. Eagle, at your service.'

That evening the crane driver poured the petrol into the tank, started the engine and swung the jib round to the right and the left and up and down. The engine hummed, the pulleys clattered, the grab rattled and everything worked as it had always done.

But apart from the crane driver and the eagle, no one knew anything about it. They were very happy and sang all night.

That autumn men came from the town with tools and lorries. They wanted to dismantle the crane. The crane driver blew his trumpet and called down: 'I'm up here.' The men were surprised to find that there was someone on the crane. They called: 'What are you doing on that old crane? Come down at once. We need the iron.'

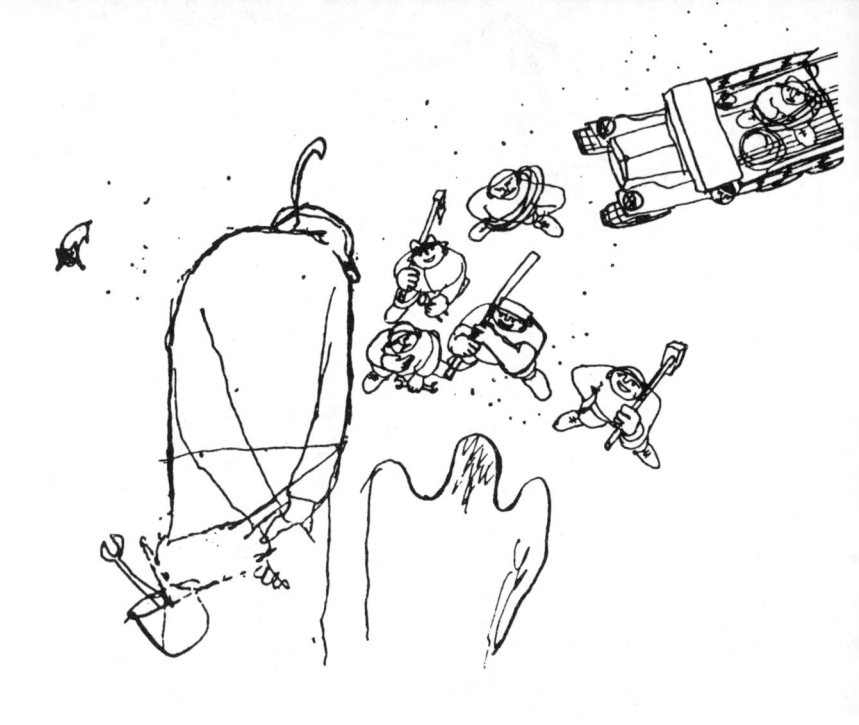

The crane driver called back: 'I was here first.'

The men shouted: 'You're crazy. Come down!'

The crane driver answered: 'I was here when it was all sea and before that when there was a harbour and a road and a railway station. I'm the crane driver.' The other men laughed at him and wanted to start unscrewing the iron girders. But the eagle dived down at them and they all ran away shouting: 'An eagle! An eagle!'

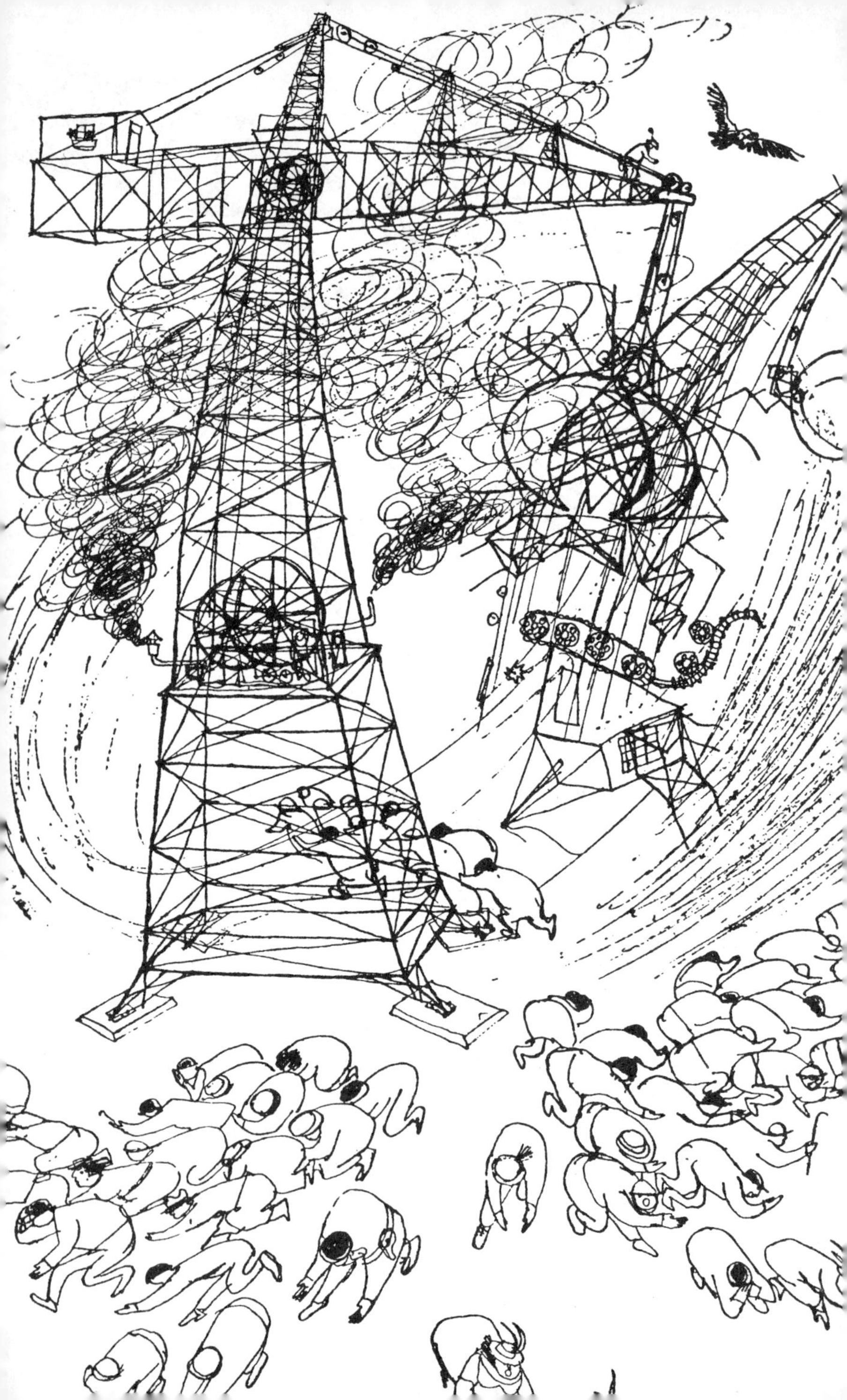

The next day they came with a dredger and wanted to dredge up the crane and the townsfolk all came too. There were as many people as there had been when the crane driver had dealt with the river pirates. He felt very proud. He put on his pirate medal and took hold of the lever. After all, he was the crane driver. He was healthy and the crane was in working order and he was going to show them. The eagle hopped from one foot to the other, he felt so pleased.

So, when they started to dredge down below, the crane driver switched on the engine and sent the grab zooming down. And the crowd yelled: 'It works! It works!' He picked up the dredger, men and all into the air with the grab and let them fall into the river as if they were toys. And because the man in charge of the dredger happened to be standing on the edge of the river bank, the eagle flew past him and pushed him into the water with his wing.

'How's that? Not bad, eh?' the crane driver said to the eagle.

That evening the town councillors met in the town hall in order to decide what to do. And since they could not think of anything better, they decided that on the following Monday the army should be sent with tanks to fetch down the crane driver.

But there was no mayor as yet, though there were two town clerks and they both wanted to be mayor. Voting was to take place next day.

When everyone had voted and the votes had been counted, it became apparent that each town clerk had exactly the same number of votes as the other.

Early on Monday morning the town councillors told the general to withdraw his troops from the crane and leave the crane driver in peace. The general sent a dispatch rider to the armoured divisions and he shouted: 'General's orders! All tanks to right about turn and withdraw from crane area.'

That afternoon the townsfolk left the town and gathered round the crane. At their head came a brass band and one of the town clerks.

First they played some music, then the town clerk shuffled his patent leather shoes in the sand and said:

'Respected friend, we have come to inform you that you will no longer be a poor man. We shall build a railway station near the crane, with twelve large halls made of glass, and ocean liners shall travel up the river—they will be painted white with yellow funnels—and all the roads in our country shall lead here. This is to be the biggest harbour in the world with a marble bridge and a thousand street lamps and we intend to build ten more cranes.'

The crowd shouted: 'Hurray!'

'And if you–er–would vote for me to be mayor, then perhaps . . .' the town clerk smiled impressively and bowed, '. . . you will be promoted to head crane superintendent at a salary of £50 a month. Do not thank me, it is nothing.' He repeated the last sentence ten times.

Then the eagle said to the crane driver: 'Pass him the trumpet.'

The crane driver shouted down: 'Can you play the trumpet?'

'I can do anything,' said the town clerk. 'What fun!' He started playing and at once drew in his head. Afterwards he said: 'Respected friend, if you vote for me I will give you a trumpet made of solid gold.'

The crane driver said: 'I'll sleep on it.' And they all marched back to town to the sound of fifes and drums and went through the streets shouting: 'Tomorrow the crane driver will choose the mayor. Three cheers for the new mayor. Hip hip hurray!' And whoever shouted loudest was given five free bottles of beer by the town clerk.

That evening the other town clerk went for a walk in the fields and came to the crane. It was already late for he had been busy in his garden after the sun had gone down sowing radishes and watering flowers.

He said to the crane driver: 'How do you do,' and sat down on the lowest girder and asked: 'What was it like here before?'

The crane driver said: 'There was a road and railway lines and there were boats on the river. And lots of trees all round.'

The town clerk whistled a tune thoughtfully. Then he said: 'First they ought to build the road and next year, the railway lines. And later on, when the ships come from the other towns, then, perhaps, also a bridge. They haven't got much money, you know, and it will all take a long time.'

'The crane's in good working order,' said the crane driver.

Then he said to the town clerk: 'Can you play the trumpet?' The town clerk replied: 'No.' And the crane driver said: 'Have a shot, anyway.' The town clerk could not manage a tune, only a few sounds, but he did not draw in his head when he played the trumpet.

Next day the crane driver voted for the town clerk with the garden to be mayor.

Everything happened as the new mayor had said it would. First they built the road, then the railway lines and that took a long time. And later on boats came from the other towns.

But when everything was finished it was just as it had been before. The crane driver sounded the siren every morning at seven and he switched on the engine. The pulley clattered and the grab clanked. The crane driver swung the jib to the right and the left and up and down and the lorries rumbled and he loaded crates and coal, cows and pigs.

When a light breeze blew from the town, the girders hummed quietly. On Sundays the crane driver went for a walk on the crane and wore the pirate medal on his chest and the baker's children came running and called up: 'Play us a tune on your trumpet.' And in winter the coal looked so black that the ravens were jealous.

The eagle circled high over the harbour and

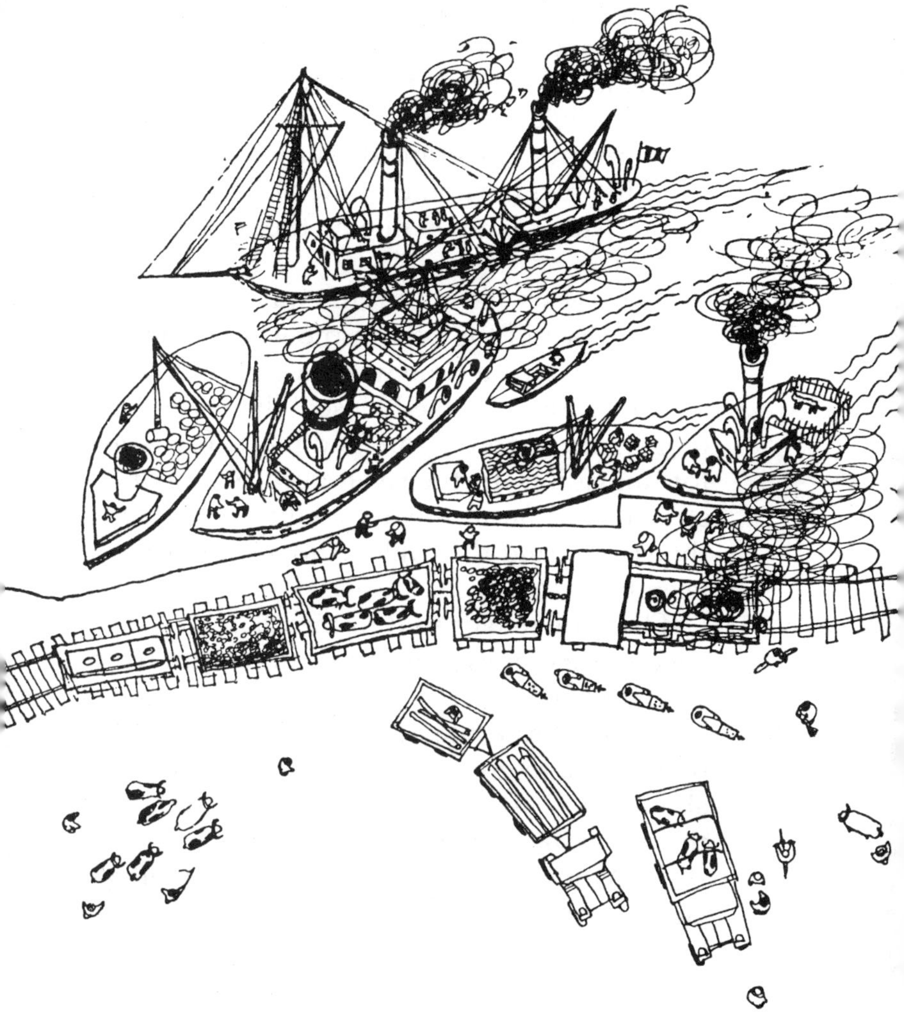

counted the lorries and ships. In the evening, after he had watered his flowers, the mayor would walk down to the crane. Then they sat on the lowest girder, the crane driver, the mayor and the eagle in the middle, each sucking a peppermint. The crane driver would describe what life had been like in the old days and the mayor would listen while he thought of his flowers.

Many years passed in this way and the crane driver was still the best in the whole country. But there came a time when a girder gave way and the screws worked loose. The town got bigger and bigger. More and more lorries arrived for unloading. In the river a procession of ships stretched as far as the eye could see. 'Nearly a thousand,' said the eagle. And a wide bridge had been built too.

Then the mayor said to the crane driver: 'We need more cranes—there are a thousand ships on their way.'

'I know,' said the old crane driver. 'And this one'll have to go,' he added quietly. 'What about you?' asked the mayor. 'I'm tired,' said the old crane driver.

On Monday men arrived with hammers and chisels and said: 'How's everything?'

And the old crane driver climbed down from the crane.

When he reached the ground it felt strange to him.

He watched them take down the girders and he saw the crane grow smaller and smaller and he said to the eagle: 'The metal is humming.'

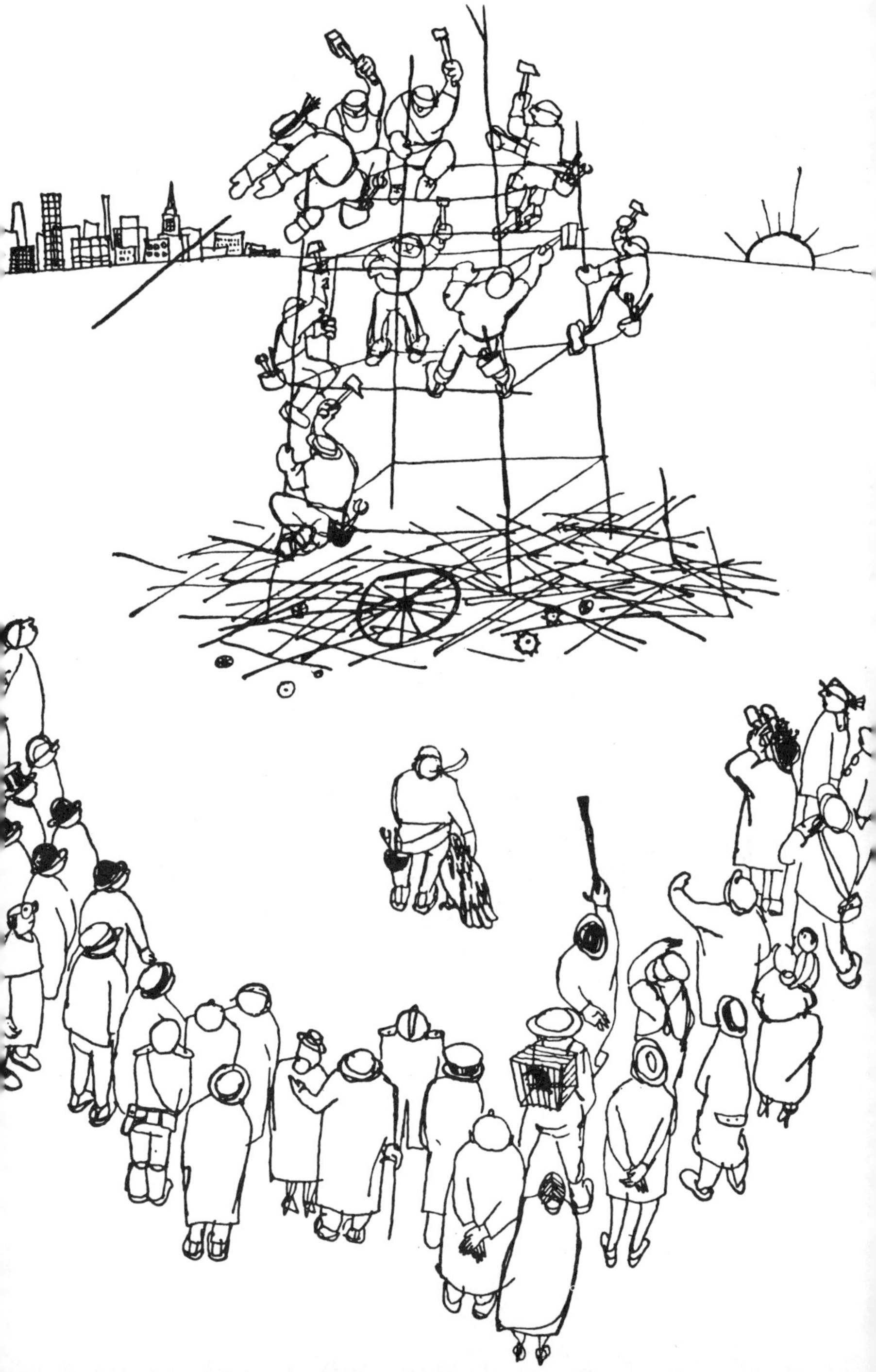

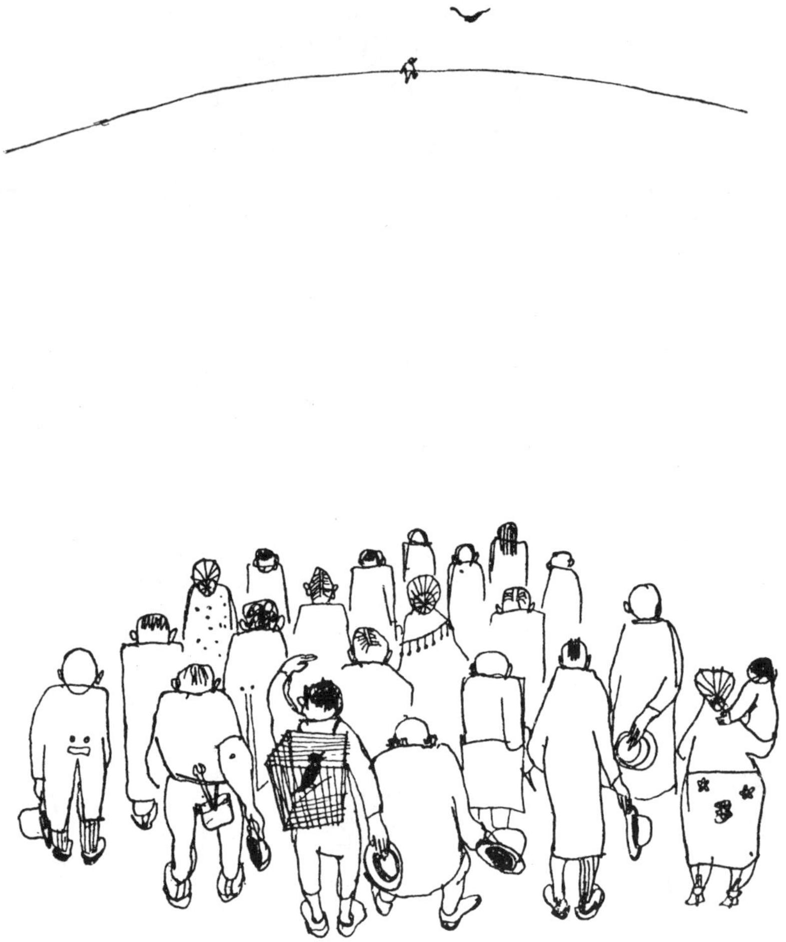

He put on his cap and said to the eagle: 'Come on!' And he walked away whistling 'Loch Lomond'. He was very tired.

When he had finished whistling it seemed as if someone else was walking beside the crane driver and the eagle. A child called out: 'Look! A silver lion!'
 The mayor said: 'That is a very wise man.'
 The crowd removed their hats and watched the crane driver. Gradually he became smaller and smaller until at last he disappeared behind the mountain.

The End.

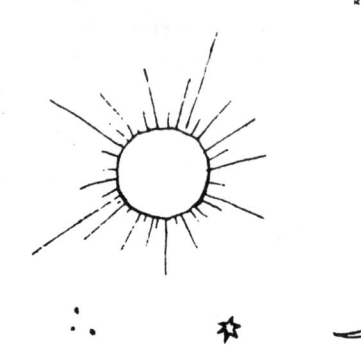